RANCH TALES

RANCH

TALES

STORIES FROM THE FRONTIER

KEN MATHER

Illustrations by ROB DINWOODIE

VICTORIA VANCOUVER CALGARY

Copyright © 2014, 2019 Ken Mather

All rights reserved. No part of this publication may be reproduced, stored in a retrieval system, or transmitted in any form or by any means—electronic, mechanical, audio recording, or otherwise—without the written permission of the publisher or a licence from Access Copyright, Toronto, Canada.

Heritage House Publishing Company Ltd.
heritagehouse.ca

Cataloguing information available from Library and Archives Canada

978-1-77203-188-1 (pbk)
978-1-77203-189-8 (ebook)

Cover and interior book design by Jacqui Thomas
Cover photograph and frontispiece: Haying crew in the South Okanagan, courtesy of the Vernon Museum
Interior illustrations by Rob Dinwoodie

The interior of this book was produced on 100% post-consumer paper, processed chlorine free and processed with vegetable-based inks.

We acknowledge the financial support of the Government of Canada through the Canada Book Fund (CBF) and the Canada Council for the Arts, and the Province of British Columbia through the British Columbia Arts Council and the Book Publishing Tax Credit.

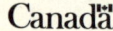   

23 22 21 20 19 1 2 3 4 5

Printed in Canada

This book is dedicated to the cowboys and ranchers of British Columbia past and present who, for a century and a half, have persevered against the forces of nature, the vicissitudes of the market, and the misunderstanding of government to make a living doing what they love to do.

<<<>>>

Contents

Author's Note ix

1 >>> The Ranching Frontier 1

2 >>> The Seventies 19

3 >>> Multiracial Families 33

4 >>> Cowboy Culture 45

5 >>> Tools of the Trade 55

6 >>> Cowboy Life 69

7 >>> Chinese Participation in the Ranching Industry 79

8 >>> Horses 87

9 >>> Ranch Women 109

10 >>> Top Hands 113

11 >>> Mud Pups 129

12 >>> Famous Ranches 139

13 >>> Ranchers 157

14 >>> Into the Twentieth Century 169

15 >>> The Cowboy in Popular Culture 177

Acknowledgements 189

Author's Note

FOR THE MOST PART, the short stories found in this book are taken from my columns, also entitled "Ranch Tales," submitted to and published periodically by the *Morning Star* newspaper in Vernon from 2007 to 2016. I have revisited all of the stories to revise and sometimes expand them in the hopes of making a more interesting and informative read, and I have added new stories where I thought it would help complete the picture. Most of the material can be found in greater detail in my three books on BC ranching history.

I am first and foremost a researcher, and I have spent a lot of time and effort with these stories to ensure their accuracy. But, despite my best attempts, there are undoubtedly some inaccuracies and mistakes.

<<< 1 >>>

The Ranching Frontier

First Cattle

IT WAS APRIL 23, 1814. There was a buzz among the grizzled North West Company fur traders who were gathered at Fort Astoria, at the mouth of the Columbia River. Their company, based in Montreal, had taken possession of the fort from the Pacific Fur Company just a few months before. On the horizon could be seen a sail of the long-awaited ship from London. The arrival of the *Isaac Todd* not only confirmed British possession of Fort Astoria and the demise of John Jacob Astor's Pacific Fur Company, it also meant "the first ship that took any Produce of the North West Company's trade collected on the west side of the Rocky Mountains." Even more curious to the Chinook people who gathered on the shore, for they had seen sailing ships before, were the animals that the *Isaac Todd* disembarked when it arrived. There were four strange animals with horns that were unlike anything the Chinooks had ever seen. To the North Westers, the two bulls and two heifers were unremarkable. Alexander Henry's journal recorded the event: "At 6.30 a boat with six men landed two young bulls and two heifers brought from San Francisco." They were the first cattle to arrive in the Pacific Northwest, the first of countless thousands that would graze on the verdant slopes and valleys of Oregon and Washington and eventually the dry bunchgrass plains of the British Columbia Interior. From this small beginning would grow an industry that would become part of the economic foundation of the Pacific Northwest.

The "two young bulls and two heifers" that the *Isaac Todd* had delivered were Spanish "blacks," the descendants of cattle brought by the Spaniards to Mexico two hundred years before. Whether these first examples of the bovine species survived or were replaced by others purchased in California is unknown. But by 1817, it was recorded that the traders at Fort George, the new name that the British Navy officers aboard the *Isaac Todd* had given the former Fort Astoria, had "about 12 head of cattle, with some pigs and goats imported here from California." The report went on to note that "their stock does not increase for want of care, the wolves often carrying off goats and pigs."

When the Hudson's Bay Company governor, George Simpson, visited Fort George in 1824, he found that the cattle herd comprised only seventeen head of cattle. This would not do. Simpson was intent on ushering in a new era of efficiency and economy in the Columbia District, one where the individual posts would produce their own vegetables and livestock for consumption. With this in mind, he moved the Hudson's Bay Company main depot on the Pacific up the Columbia River, opposite and just upriver from the mouth of the Willamette River, where it was better situated to grow and raise its own produce. Simpson enthused that, at Fort Vancouver, "We selected a beautiful point on the south side … an excellent Farm can be made at this place where as much Grain and potatoes may be raised as well would feed all the Indigenous people of the Columbia and sufficient number of Cattle and Hogs to supply His Majesty's Navy with Beef and Pork." The cattle industry in the Pacific Northwest had truly begun.

The Beginning of Ranching

FORT KAMLOOPS HUMMED WITH EXCITEMENT. In the east could be seen clouds of dust from the hooves of about two hundred pack horses. The annual fur brigade was approaching the fort, bringing the precious trade goods that were the life blood of the fur trade. The pack horses carried not just pots, pans, and guns but, even more important, tea, sugar, flour, and tobacco. As the brigade drew close to the fort, the Shuswap people stared wide-eyed at a handful of strange animals that were travelling along with the pack horses. These large animals had horns somewhat like a mountain goat but were different from anything the Shuswaps had seen before. The seasoned Hudson's Bay men smiled at their amazement and explained, "Those are cattle, and you will love the meat from them." The first cattle had arrived in the British Columbia Interior and, from these few head, an industry would grow that would supply a livelihood for hundreds of families and food for countless thousands.

The year was 1833. In its ongoing effort to make each post self-sufficient, the Hudson's Bay Company was introducing cattle to the interior of New Caledonia, the area that roughly covered what now is known as British Columbia. The strategic location of Fort Kamloops on the Brigade Trail made it essential that it produce enough to supply the passing fur brigades as well as its own employees. It was found that cattle thrived on the excellent bunchgrass ranges in the area. An examination of the Fort journals for the 1850s indicates a significant amount of activity in raising cattle and horses. Employees were busy harvesting hay, moving animals from one pasture to another, branding horses and cattle, castrating calves and horses, building stables, and killing oxen. The natural increase of the herd was such that by 1859, Fort Kamloops was slaughtering eight head of cattle every ten days to supply the needs of passing gold miners.

By the 1850s, the Company at Fort Kamloops was using local Shuswap people as herders, drovers, agricultural workers, and packers. Their experience in raising horses, their nearby proximity, and their willingness to work made them the logical choice to take over the duties of caring for and driving the cattle. Their horse-riding equipment revealed the influence of the Spanish packers who worked for the Hudson's Bay Company. Lieutenant Mayne of the Royal Engineers came through the Lillooet area in 1858–59 and described how the Indigenous People "copied the Spanish wooden saddle for riding and made bridles of simple cord or often of the hair of the wild sheep for it cannot be called wool, plaited. The middle of this is passed through the horse's mouth and hitched around its lower jaw and the ends brought up on each side of his neck."

This tendency to hire Indigenous people for cattle and horse tending would prove to be one of the unique aspects of ranching in British Columbia. The ranching industry has remained an "equal opportunity" employer where both Indigenous and non-Indigenous people were judged more for their ability to ride and tend cattle than by the colour of their skin.

The Cariboo Trail

GOLD WAS DISCOVERED ALONG THE Fraser and Thompson Rivers in the mid-1850s and, in 1858, there was a rush of would-be miners to the lower Fraser River. Although gold was found there in paying quantities, the general opinion was that the source of the gold was upriver, north of the perilous Fraser Canyon. So the more adventurous miners began to work their way up the precipitous walls of the Canyon and, having reached the mouth of the Thompson River, found even coarser gold above the Canyon. Before long the mining frontier had advanced into the area that came to be called the Cariboo.

Getting supplies to the miners above the Fraser Canyon was a great challenge. The Canyon was only passable by men carrying packs and gave little hope to become the main supply route to the Upper Fraser. The Colonial Government, realizing this, began the construction of a series of trails to connect the chain of lakes from Harrison Lake to the Fraser at Lillooet.

While this route was completed by late 1858, the combination of water and trail transport made it slow and expensive for freight.

But there was another route into the Interior that was tried in 1858. This involved using the old Hudson's Bay Company Brigade Trail from the Columbia River in Washington Territory through the Okanagan Valley to Fort Kamloops and then, from there, down the Thompson River to the Fraser. The cattlemen of Western Oregon, who saw the opportunity to dispose of their surplus cattle in the new goldfields, realized this route as the best and easiest way to get their cattle to the new market.

From the Willamette River Valley, cattle were either trailed through the mountain passes of the Cascades or loaded on steamboats and transported to The Dalles on the eastern side of the Cascade Mountains. Between the Cascades and the Rocky Mountains were rich grazing lands where the cattle could range freely until it was time to drive them north over what came to be known as the Cariboo Trail—not to be confused with the Cariboo Road, which was constructed between 1862 and 1865.

The two main departure points to reach the British Columbia mines were The Dalles, a steamboat port on the Columbia River, and Walla Walla, built near the site of the abandoned Whitman missionary station and the US military post, Fort Walla Walla.

From The Dalles, there were two possible routes of travel. Drovers could cross the Columbia River and travel by way of Fort Simcoe to Priests Rapids, where they crossed the Columbia again; or they could stay on the west side of the Columbia all the way to the Okanogan River. From Walla Walla, the trail led across the Snake River and north via the Grand Coulee to the Columbia River, which was crossed at the mouth of the Okanogan River.

From Fort Okanogan, cattle were driven along the old Hudson's Bay Company Brigade Trail on the east side of the Okanogan River. After crossing the border at Osoyoos Lake, the Brigade Trail led along the west side of Okanagan Lake and then over the height of land to Fort Kamloops. Staying south of Kamloops Lake, it crossed the Thompson River at the west end of the lake by means of a cable ferry operated by a former Hudson's Bay Company employee, Francois Saveneau. English-speaking drovers pronounced the ferryman's name "Savona," and the town that grew up at the site of his ferry has kept the same name. Cattle were normally swum across the river at this point, while pack horses and men rode the ferry. The trail continued west until it reached the Bonaparte River and then proceeded to the Fraser and on to Barkerville in the heart of the Cariboo goldfields. Through its entire eight-hundred-mile length, this route had the great advantage of travelling through rich grasslands, making it possible to keep the cattle in excellent condition as they headed north.

The trail was not without its hazards. Swimming the cattle across the Columbia River, especially at Priests Rapids, could be extremely dangerous for cattle and drovers alike. Many drovers lost cattle on these crossings, watching them disappear downstream, never to be recovered. As well, for those who stayed on the west side of the Columbia to avoid two river crossings, the precipitous cliffs north of present-day Wenatchee presented an equal potential for disaster. Cattle were lost so frequently on this stretch that the local Indigenous people regularly patrolled the river to pick up the bodies. Added to these hazards were the almost constant mosquitoes that plagued cattle, horses, and drovers alike. Maddened cattle would charge off the trail into the lake or river or, even worse, over a cliff or into a canyon. Other hazards included wolves and poisonous plants, such as water hemlock, not to mention the extreme heat or pouring rain that made the journey far from easy. Every mile of the trail had its challenges, and the drovers had to be on constant alert to the dangers that surrounded them.

Nevertheless, between 1858 and 1868, over 22,000 head of cattle were driven up the Cariboo Trail, across the border at Osoyoos, and into the British Columbia Interior. Many of the drovers stayed and began cattle ranching on the bunchgrass ranges of the Interior and founded the British Columbia cattle industry.

The Epic Journey of Joel Palmer

JOEL PALMER WAS A GRIZZLED veteran of battles with Indigenous People and with first-hand experience of the harshness of frontier life. He had been born to Quaker parents on Canada's Lake Ontario. After various endeavours in the eastern United States, he travelled the overland trail to the Oregon Country (as the area was then referred to) in 1845. Palmer's natural ability as a leader of men was soon recognized in Oregon Territory. In 1847, he became the commissary general of an expedition to the Palouse region in southeastern Washington Territory to rescue the women and children who had been captured after the massacre at the Whitman Mission. People subsequently referred to him as "General Palmer," a title that he accepted with great pleasure. Palmer even looked like a general with his powerful commanding figure and deep-set, penetrating eyes.

Palmer was fiercely loyal to the territory of Oregon, which had become his home. He was determined to see it prosper and become a state in the US. But the area lacked markets for the livestock and agricultural produce from the rich river valleys east of the Cascade Mountains. In the spring of 1858, Palmer travelled north from Walla Walla with thirteen heavily laden wagons and a small herd of cattle. He and his party crossed the Snake River and headed toward the Columbia River. It was hard going through the sand hills north of the Snake River, but after the Grand Coulee, things were easier. Crossing the wide Columbia at the mouth of the Okanogan River with thirteen wagons presented a real challenge to the intrepid Palmer, but once again, he displayed his characteristic ingenuity. He negotiated with the Indigenous people living there for the use of canoes and, lashing two canoes together side by side, rolled the wagons onto the canoes and paddled them across the Columbia in safety.

Palmer proceeded up the Brigade Trail through the Okanagan Valley, widening the trail with axe and saw wherever necessary. He and his party eventually reached the Fraser River mines and disposed of their cattle and wagons at a profit. Over the next two years, Palmer made several trips up the

Trail, choosing pack horses instead of wagons to carry his goods, and driving cattle, or "beeves" as they were referred to at the time, to the mines of the Cariboo. He never lost an opportunity to tell his fellow Oregonians about the potential markets in British Columbia, and wrote to the editor of the *Oregonian* newspaper in January 1860: "With a comparatively small outlay in improving the wagon routes between points of steam navigation the cost of transporting supplies would be lessened to such an extent as would give to us much of the carrying trade, thereby securing as an outlet for the products of our valleys. It is evident that if trade continues by way of Victoria and [the] Fraser River, nearly all supplies will be purchased, as they have been, in San Francisco."

His words obviously made an impact on the cattlemen of Oregon and California—the next ten years were to see a constant flow of cattle northward into British Columbia and 22,000 head of cattle cross the border at Osoyoos.

The Incredible Harper Brothers

THE HARPER BROTHERS, JEROME AND Thaddeus, were "larger than life" cattlemen who did everything in a big way—including the acquisition of land. From their small beginnings as drovers, they quickly became the largest landowners in British Columbia, pre-empting and purchasing thousands of acres of prime grazing land throughout the Interior. The shrewd Harpers did not restrict their entrepreneurial interests to the cattle business, with interests in sawmills, flour mills, slaughterhouses, and mines in various BC locations.

The Harpers were from Virginia and lifelong sympathizers with the Confederate cause. They had spent some time in California ranching and mining before they heard of gold being discovered in British Columbia. Seeing the opportunity for a new market for their cattle, they began to drive cattle from California all the way to the new colony. Before long they were the largest importers of cattle into BC and, with the encouragement of the colonial government, began to acquire land in the rich bunchgrass ranges of the Interior.

As early as 1862, Jerome occupied land east of Kamloops on the north side of the Thompson River, which formed the nucleus of what is still known as the Harper Ranch, eventually totalling 3,957 acres. As their cattle interests grew, the Harpers purchased several other large tracts of lands closer to the Cariboo market, where the brothers had interests in a slaughterhouse near Barkerville. In 1867, they bought 216 acres at Quesnelle Mouth (present-day Quesnel), and four years later, the brothers secured the Perry Ranch near Cache Creek. Later they acquired Edward Kelly's ranch in the Cut Off Valley near Clinton and, in January 1873, Jerome Harper took over the mortgage on Hat Creek Ranch on the Cariboo Road, just north of Cache Creek. This famous stopping house, which still stands next to Highway 97, was leased out to various operators who paid an annual rent, and the Harpers used the land for holding cattle.

Thaddeus Harper became the manager of the brothers' interests in British Columbia when Jerome left the colony in the early 1870s. Jerome contracted a severe illness and was forced to seek expert medical attention in San Francisco. The city offered a number of temptations for a young man with unlimited finances, and Jerome indulged fully, perhaps knowing that his time was limited. In December 1874, Jerome was found dead in a bathtub.

The Harpers' greatest land purchase, and part of their enduring legacy, was the acquisition of the lands that came to be known as the Gang Ranch. The area seems isolated now, but in the early gold rush days, the first trail into the Cariboo was via Lillooet along the "River Trail" on the east side of the Fraser River. During the early 1860s, the Harpers had held their cattle in this area and took up land on Dog Creek Mountain. The vast stretches of grasslands across the Fraser probably caught their entrepreneurial eyes, but the inaccessibility of the area made them hesitate. Cattle would have to be driven across the Fraser River to the main roads and trails before travelling to market. By 1884, when Thaddeus Harper purchased 18,912 acres of land from the government in the Chilcotin district, the Gang Ranch was well established.

Unfortunately, like his brother Jerome, Thaddeus's life was to end tragically. He was kicked in the face by a horse on the Gang Ranch and never fully recovered from the severe head injuries. He died in Victoria in 1898.

The Jeffries Brothers

JOHN AND OLIVER JEFFRIES WERE from Alabama and came to the Pacific Northwest in the 1850s to look for gold. Hearing about the market for cattle in British Columbia due to the gold rush, John Jeffries purchased cattle in Oregon in the fall of 1860 and drove them up the Cariboo Trail to the Upper Fraser River. The daily journal for October 1, 1860, kept by the Hudson's Bay Company at Fort Kamloops recorded "a large band of cattle arrived from the Dalls [sic]" in charge of "a Mr. Jefferies." After holding the cattle in the Bonaparte River area until they were needed, Jeffries was able to sell them all at a reasonable profit. Encouraged by the prospects for the following year, he returned to Oregon to buy another large herd the following spring. In partnership with his brother, Oliver, Jeffries returned to British Columbia. In March 1861, Judge Cox wrote to Governor Douglas that "a Mr. Jeffries is approaching with 800 head I understand, and will if possible, control the beef market in the upper country."

During the summer of 1861, John and Oliver Jeffries had driven a herd of cattle as far as Bridge Creek, at the 100 Mile post on the trail from Lillooet. Seeing the advantage of pasturing their cattle on the abundant grasslands in the area before driving them into the Cariboo goldfields, they decided to establish a ranch. In partnership with Thomas Miller, J.E. Johnstone and Reinhardt, the Jeffries brothers took up land at Bridge Creek and, for the next few years, were continually conveying land back and forth between them. They built Bridge Creek House in 1861. Known as "Jeffries Store," the single-story, squared-log structure contained a barroom and kitchen, and a sleeping area in the attic. Bishop Hills, in a diary entry of July 10, 1862, described his visit to Bridge Creek: "At Bridge Creek was a band of cattle driven in from Oregon by the brother of Jeffries. He places at various points droves of cattle. Here one of them keeps a store. Mr. Knipe and I had dinner there today. For a beefsteak and coffee the charge was a dollar and a half. I also bought for my party 10 lbs of beef at 45 cents a lb. We camped about a mile south of the House, and sent our horses across the stream to a bench where was an excellent feed of Bunchgrass."

In 1862, the Fort Kamloops journal recorded John Jeffries as having arrived with "upwards of 700 head" of horned cattle.

Like his fellow Southerner, Jerome Harper, Jeffries was aggressive in his attempt to control the beef market. Perhaps his cleverest attempt at turning away competitors is shown in a letter from John Carmichael Haynes, who had taken over from Cox as the Customs Agent at Osoyoos Lake, to the Colonial Secretary in August of 1863:

> "I have been told by a Mr. Murphy who passed this station ... that several cattle dealers having herds for this country were prevented from starting owing to reports circulated by a Mr. Jeffries and other interested persons to the effect that all livestock intended for this country would be stopped on the frontier by officers of the United States Government placed there for that purpose. Mr. Murphy also mentions that he heard Mr. Jeffries state publicly at Walla Walla that I had told him. I have not seen Mr. Jeffries for over a year ... Mr. Harper who entered a drove of cattle on the 20th inst. [instant, i.e. "day of the month"] told me that several stock owners were waiting in the vicinity of Walla Walla to ascertain as to whether they could 'get thru' or not."

Jeffries was nothing if not clever, for his story had a basis in truth. In late 1862, the United States government, as a Civil War measure, had passed an embargo on all livestock leaving the country. This embargo was never enforced in the Pacific Northwest, and in September 1863 was modified to permit the export of "stock raised in a state or territory bordered on the Pacific Ocean." Nonetheless, the embargo, along with Jeffries' story, discouraged many drovers from heading north, and the Jeffries and Harper brothers saw significant profits that year.

Unlike the Harper brothers, who remained in British Columbia after the Cariboo gold rush was over, the Jeffries brothers sold their assets and left the colony, perhaps returning to their beloved south after the Civil War.

British Columbia's First Ranch

THE QUESTION IS OFTEN ASKED, "Just which ranch is the oldest one in British Columbia?" Although various ranches have been suggested over the years, it is now generally accepted that the first ranch in BC (and one that is still in operation) is the Alkali Lake Ranch.

Like many of the "firsts" in BC history, the origins of the ranch can be traced to the early years of the gold rush. As miners searched for richer gold diggings, they worked their way up the Fraser River and by 1859 had penetrated past the precipitous Fraser Canyon into the area that came to be called the Cariboo. In the spring of that year, a miner named Lewis Cardis discovered fair diggings on a gravel bar just south of where the Chilcotin River enters the Fraser. Among the miners who arrived at Cardis Bar, as it was called, was Herman Otto Bowe, who had been born in Hamburg, Germany, and left home as a young man to look for gold in California.

While Bowe was somewhat successful mining at Cardis Bar, he was more impressed with the surrounding country that was covered in lush bunchgrass. After trying his hand at mining farther into the Cariboo, he returned to the area and set up a little trading post, saloon, and roadhouse at a location he called Paradise Valley. The stopping house was next to Alkali Lake, named after the white deposits in the area. In 1861, in partnership with another young man, Phillip Grinder, he pre-empted (the term for homesteading in those days) 360 acres of rich grasslands surrounding his stopping house ... and the Alkali Lake Ranch was born.

To stock the ranch, Bowe purchased a herd of ragged, skin-and-bone cattle that had barely survived the long drive up from Oregon. The cattle were sold by L.W. Riske (pronounced RISkee), and his partners, Sam and Ed Withrow, all destined to be pioneers in the Chilcotin. Before long, the cattle were fat and flourishing on the bunchgrass range, and with his share of the profits, Bowe was able to purchase Phil Grinder's half of the ranch.

<<<>>>

BY 1865, THE NEW CARIBOO Road, which bypassed Alkali Lake, was finished and the need for a stopping house disappeared. But Bowe continued to raise cattle and supply the goldfields with fat beef. He married Caroline Belleau, daughter of the Alkali Lake chief, and the two settled down to make a home. During the 1870s, when markets for beef dwindled, Bowe took a new business partner, John Koster, to help with the ranch, and together they purchased more land and more cattle. The ranch prospered under their management and as they grew older, their children were able to take over more of the operation.

In 1909, the Alkali Lake Ranch was sold to C. Wynn Johnson, and Otto Bowe retired, eventually passing away in New Westminster in 1912. But the Alkali Lake Ranch continues to carry on the tradition of cattle ranching and can claim the dual honour of being the first cattle ranch and the longest continually operating ranch in the province.

The Confederate Cattlemen

VIRGINIAN BROTHERS JEROME AND THADDEUS HARPER were fast friends with their fellow Southerners and drovers, John and Oliver Jeffries. When the American Civil War erupted in the east in 1861, they became fierce believers in the right of the Confederate States to separate from the Union.

Many of the drovers were American, so the strong feelings caused by the bitter war between the states provoked much heated exchange along the trail. Mostly though, the strong hand of British justice, embodied in the formidable judge, Matthew Baillie Begbie, kept a lid on hostilities, and drovers simply avoided those with opposing points of view.

Once the Jeffries brothers had established themselves as major beef suppliers, they preferred to spend their winters in Victoria, living with a large number of Southern sympathizers in the St. Nicholas Hotel on Government Street. During the winter of 1862–63, emotions between the Southerners and Unionists reached a fever pitch and, as the rebel victories mounted during those months, a number of incidents showed just how much the animosity had built up. On one occasion, the American eagle on the coat of arms on the American Consulate in Victoria had a black "stovepipe" hat and pipe painted on it. The next day, a small Confederate flag was flown over one of the shops in downtown Victoria. A determined party of Unionists who marched on the shop was met by twenty or thirty Confederate sympathizers, among them, no doubt, the Jeffries brothers. For a time, until those with a modicum of wisdom on both sides intervened, a pitched battle seemed inevitable.

During this period, the Jeffries brothers, Jerome Harper, and others hit upon the scheme of fitting out a privateer ship to prey on American shipping out of San Francisco, especially the treasure ship that left San Francisco twice a month with two to three million dollars in gold destined for the east. The intention was to intercept, rob, and burn steamers along the lonely Mexican coast and escape with the treasure. This scheme had advanced to the stage where Jefferson Davis and Confederate Secretary of State

Judah P. Benjamin signed "letters of marque" effectively authorizing such activities for the Jeffries brothers and their fellow conspirators. They recruited an officer and crew from among the Southerners in Victoria and located a suitable ship.

The conspiracy failed at the last moment when Richard Lovell, who had been masquerading as a Southern sympathizer on behalf of the Union, stole the papers containing all the details. Lovell was discovered and severely beaten by John Jeffries, but the word was out. Thanks to Lovell's information, Allen Francis, the American Consul in Victoria, was able to defuse the scheme. When a steamship carrying four guns, the *Shurbrick*, arrived from across the Puget Sound and pulled into Esquimalt harbour, the ship was met by Union authorities and all but two officers were discharged for suspected disloyalty. The intention had been to take over the *Shurbrick* and convert her into a privateer under the sponsorship of the Jeffries, the Harpers, and their friends, but the scheme was thwarted. The discovery of this conspiracy greatly discouraged the Confederate sympathizers in British Columbia and, aside from a few minor incidents, the war ran its bloody course without involving the colony in any significant way.

Stopping Houses on the Cariboo Road

THE CARIBOO GOLD RUSH YEARS of 1858 to 1868 saw thousands of would-be miners flock to the BC Interior and changed the landscape forever. Roadside ranches sprung up all along the Cariboo Road and other routes into the Interior. Enterprising drovers settled on land along the road, seizing the opportunity to prosper by supplying food and lodging to the miners, freighters, and stagecoaches streaming to the goldfields. Many of the drovers, especially those along the Cariboo Road, established stopping houses to profit from the steady stream of miners and other adventurers on their way to and from the Cariboo. The "mile houses," as they were called, were named for the distance they were located from "Mile Zero" at Lillooet and were scattered along the Cut Off Valley to Clinton and along the Cariboo Wagon Road. The owners produced their own crops and usually kept a herd of cattle to supply fresh beef to their patrons, making these the very first ranches in the BC Interior. Many of these names are still with us today, as in 100 Mile House and the 108 Mile Ranch.

150 Mile Stopping House

THE 150 MILE HOUSE, one of the earliest stopping houses along the way, served as the social centre for the ranchers in the area as well as a roadhouse. Beginning in the gold rush days, it was one of the major stops on the way to the goldfields and had prospered under various owners. Like most stopping houses in those days, it had no central heating, with all the heat being supplied from heaters on the main floor that had stovepipes extending through the roof. This meant that the upstairs rooms could be extremely cold in the winter. During very cold weather, guests were brought a pre-breakfast hot toddy to help ignite the internal fires.

Alvin Johnston of Quesnel stayed in the hotel on one particularly cold December night. Since the hotel was quite full, he was given a small room at the very back of the upstairs. Despite consuming numerous hot rums before retiring, Johnston spent a long night huddled in his bed trying to stay warm. When morning finally arrived, he rushed downstairs to warm up beside the main heater. A few minutes earlier, an early-morning traveller had arrived at the hotel, completely swaddled in outdoor clothing and with long icicles hanging from his moustache. As he stood beside the stove, Johnston took one look at him and asked, "My God, which room did you have?"

Many of the stopping houses in the British Columbia Interior were eventually destroyed by fire, often caused by faulty chimneys or overturned oil lamps, and the 150 Mile House was no exception. It burned to the ground in the early morning of February 13, 1916. Fortunately, there was no loss of life but there was one near tragedy. Alex Meiss of Horsefly had to flee his room without his most prized possession: his wooden leg. While being carried to safety by the hotel manager, Alex shouted that his wooden leg was still in the burning building. Spurred by Alex's cries, an intrepid hero rushed into the building through the smoke and flames and successfully rescued the leg. The Cariboo Trading Company did not rebuild the hotel but continued to operate the store until 1928.

<<< **2** >>>

The Seventies

Driving Horses through the Yellowhead Pass

THE 1870S WERE A TIME of stagnation for the ranchers of the new province of British Columbia as the gold rush activity dwindled and the promised railway connection with the rest of Canada stalled. Various attempts were made to alleviate the overcrowded ranges of cattle and horses, but none more enterprising than the scheme of Adam Ferguson and James Christie. Ferguson, thirty-two years old, was originally from Scotland, and Christie, twenty years old, from Ireland. The two decided that there ought to be a market for horses in the Red River area, some two thousand kilometers to the east. They knew that there was a trail up the North Thompson River and through the Yellowhead Pass that avoided the prairies where the Blackfoot still ruled supreme. The two men purchased 107 head of horses from the BX Ranch in the North Okanagan and, on July 7, 1874, headed up the North Thompson.

Although survey parties for the promised Canadian Pacific Railway had struggled through the Yellowhead Pass as part of their explorations, the trail was seldom used, blocked by deadfall and overgrown with bush, especially on the part that ran from the North Thompson River to Tête Jaune Cache on the headwaters of the Fraser River. Ferguson and

Christie made good time as far as the old Hudson's Bay Company post of Little Fort, at the mouth of the Clearwater River. From there, the trail deteriorated and eventually disappeared. It was one thing for a man on horseback to navigate the deadfall and bush, but driving a herd of wild horses through it was incredibly difficult. Ferguson and Christie had to chop their way through, and progress slowed to a crawl until they reached Tête Jaune Cache.

From there, the Yellowhead Pass itself was open and relatively easy going until they reached Jasper House. The trail from there was every bit as difficult as the one they had already traversed. It passed through 220 miles of spruce forest and swamp. In places, the men had to go ahead with axes to cut a way through the deadfall. Horses sank up to their chests in the mud and swamp and had to be pulled out with ropes or pried out of the mud with poles. They were also confronted with several major river crossings. The Pembina River, some 160 metres wide, was one of the toughest. They watched with despair as horses lost footing and disappeared into the rapid current, some not to be seen again. But there remained no other option but to push forward.

By September 26, they had reached Lac St. Anne, a Metis outpost and mission some 50 miles from Fort Edmonton. Of the original 107 horses, there remained 72, most in terrible condition. After resting there for a few days, the men drove the horses on to Fort Edmonton. Recognizing that the size and strength of the horses surpassed anything on the prairies, the Chief Factor at the fort purchased the entire band from Ferguson and Christie, saving them from driving the horses another 840 miles farther to the Red River.

Adam Ferguson took his hard-earned money and returned to British Columbia, while Jim Christie went to Montana and purchased more horses to drive into the ranching country around Fort Macleod. He became the "Pioneer Horseman" of Alberta and settled in the area. Many BC horses were to come to the prairies but none via such a difficult route as these two frontiersmen had taken.

Cattle across the Great Divide

STRANGE AS IT MAY SEEM, the first cattle to arrive in Calgary, the centre of ranching in Canada and home of the Stampede, came from British Columbia! A man by the name of John Shaw bears the distinction of being the first man to bring cattle for stock-raising purposes to the Canadian prairies. Little is known of John Shaw except for this incredible drive through the Rocky Mountains. What we do know about Shaw is that he was one of the first miners on the scene to mine gold at Stud Horse Creek (later named Wild Horse Creek with true Victorian sensitivity) in 1864. The creek was located in the East Kootenay area, known as the Columbia Lakes district.

The creek produced large quantities of gold for a couple years but, by 1868 the area was mined out and miners headed off to the next gold excitement. Shaw was taken with the country and decided to stay, pre-empting land on the Kootenay River and buying up cattle that were selling for rock-bottom prices. On the lush bottomlands, his cattle thrived but the dwindling market meant that he had more cattle than money. Shaw hung on to his land, finally selling it in 1874 to the Oblate priest, Father Foquet, who set up St. Eugene Mission on the land. The priest was not interested in the cattle, and Shaw looked anxiously for a market. He heard that the North West Mounted Police had come to the prairies across the Rocky Mountains and had pacified the mighty Blackfoot. So Shaw decided to round up his cattle and drive them to Fort Edmonton, some 350 miles away.

Shaw found two good cowboys in Frank O'Keefe and Charles Ashton, both from the North Okanagan. Frank was the brother of rancher Cornelius O'Keefe, and Charles Ashton had taken up land in the North Okanagan in 1866. Whether they were in the Kootenays prospecting or Shaw had travelled to the Okanagan is uncertain, but the two would have been valuable additions to the mostly Kootenay crew. However the meeting came about, in the spring of 1875 the men headed out with a herd of 389 head of cattle and enough horses that the men could switch mounts if they so desired.

The next challenge was to pick a way through the barrier of the Rocky Mountains. It has been suggested that Shaw took the Crowsnest Pass, but at that time it was overgrown and impassable. When Thomas Blakiston of the Palliser Expedition had passed through the area in 1858, searching for a pass through the mountains suitable for a railway, he noted that "by report of the natives it is a very hard road, and seldom used." Shaw and his drove would probably have chosen the North Kootenay Pass, which had been used for centuries by the Kootenay people to pass through the mountains to the prairies.

They proceeded south along the Kootenay River to Tobacco Plains and then turned east to the opening of the North Kootenay Pass. At the start of the trail, there was good water and pasture, so the cattle were allowed time to graze and fatten up for the push over the pass. From there the trail ascended gradually but steadily until it reached the top of the Great Divide. The trail was well marked, as the Kootenay people had used it that spring to travel to the prairies. At the top of the pass, the trail passed through alpine vegetation growing low to the ground, and there was still snow on the ground. The trail then started to descend and before long, they were on relatively level ground and headed out on to the prairies. But there remained another three hundred miles to Fort Edmonton.

The drive was slow going through the mountains and made slower because many of the cows were calving. Shaw did not want to lose marketable cattle and kept the calves with their mothers, even though it slowed things down. Now that they were on the edge of the prairies, the grasslands were extensive and the cattle were allowed to graze their way along, averaging twelve to fifteen miles a day. Charles Ashton later told his daughter Minnie the story of the variable weather they encountered on the way.

> Although my father was not given to reminiscences, I have heard him tell how on that trip on the prairies as they rode herd, they were on one night nearly eaten alive with mosquitoes and on the next they had struck a blizzard that almost froze them in their saddles.

The cattle drive proceeded without incident and reached the little settlement of Morley on about August 10. George McDougall and his extended family had just arrived in the Bow River Valley. Shortly after they arrived, the Hudson's Bay Company had established a post at the same location under the supervision of John Bunn.

Shaw intended to stay at Morley for a few days before heading on his way to Fort Edmonton. However, John McDougall informed him that there was likely little to no market for cattle at the Fort and suggested he winter his cattle at Morley.

Shaw then approached Bunn to see if he was interested in purchasing the cattle or if his superiors at Fort Edmonton would consider it. Bunn doubted that there was a demand for cattle at Fort Edmonton but agreed to write to his superior, Chief Factor Richard Hardisty. In a letter dated August 14 he wrote,

> Mr. John Shaw from Kootenai arrived here the other day with a band of 450 head of cattle, his intention was to have gone on to Edmonton to sell them but he was told that there was not sale for more than 30 or 40 head at most & therefore he has decided to winter them here—he has some good looking 3 & 4 year old steers included and I asked him what his price was for such. He said $60 & $70! That shut me up.

After further discussion with Shaw, Bunn added a postscript to the letter. "After closing my letter to you, Mr. Shaw called on me to say that he will sell out his whole stock including 9 horses for $38.00 a head, not including 60 spring calves which he will throw in." Unfortunately, the Hudson's Bay Company had no market or need for the cattle, buffalo still being abundant on the prairies. So Shaw decided to winter his cattle in the Morley area and hope that spring would bring some outlet for his cattle.

When the spring of 1876 arrived, John Shaw found with some surprise that his cattle had survived the winter well and, even though they had lost some weight, they soon fattened up on the lush grasses of the foothills. There was still no indication that Fort Edmonton was interested in beef. But, down the Bow River a few miles, at the junction with the Elbow River, there was a flurry of activity where Colonel Macleod of the the North West Mounted Police had instructed Inspector Ephrem Brisbois to establish a fort for the Mounted Police. D.W. Davis, the Canadian representative of I.G. Baker and Company, was given the contract to construct the fort. He hired a crew of Metis and Americans from Fort Macleod to do the work and, by winter, a fort measuring 150 square feet had been hastily completed, with quarters for the men on the west side, shops and storerooms on the east side, officers' quarters and a guardhouse on the south, and stables on the north. That fall, John Bunn relocated the Hudson's Bay Company post next to the fort. I.G. Baker and Company also built a trading post, and T.C. Power & Brother constructed a store next to the fort. The little settlement was further enhanced with a billiard hall operated by Harry "Kamoose" Taylor and a group of Metis cabins.

I.G. Baker and Company had also been contracted to supply the Fort with provisions but was reluctant to drive cattle all the way from Montana. When D.W. Davis learned that Shaw was holding almost four hundred head of cattle just down the river at Morley, he subcontracted Shaw to provide beef cattle to the Mounted Police. And so, in the spring of 1876, the first beef cattle were driven into the little settlement that was to become Calgary, as it was named by Colonel Macleod of the Mounted Police. Little did the inhabitants know that the dusty little community would someday become the centre of Canada's ranching industry.

Shaw and his cowboys were kept busy through the summer driving beef, a few at a time, to the little NWMP post. The cattle sold at an excellent profit. John Shaw, ever the adventurer, decided to keep going on to Fort Edmonton, and the rest of his life is lost to history. But his cowboys turned around and headed back to the Okanagan.

Epic Cattle Drive of 1876

THE BEST-KNOWN AND, WITHOUT A DOUBT, longest drive out of British Columbia in the early days was organized by Thaddeus Harper in the spring of 1876. Harper purchased about eight hundred head of cattle, from three- to eight-years-old, in the Dog Creek, Canoe Creek, and Alkali Lake areas. The age of these cattle gives a clear indication of just how overstocked the ranges had become during the economic doldrums of the 1870s, cattle normally selling for slaughter as three-year olds. By May 16, they were reported to have reached a point "a little above Clinton, bound for Salt Lake City." Under the leadership of trail boss, Newman Squires, the cattle were moved slowly, averaging about twelve miles a day and grazing on the spring grass along the route. At the O'Keefe Ranch, the cattle rested a few days and an additional 428 head were purchased from the ranchers in the area. The drive continued through the Okanagan Valley and crossed the border into Washington State at Osoyoos, eventually crossing the Snake River near Walla Walla. By then, winter was approaching and Harper decided to winter his cattle and wait to see market conditions in the spring.

Most of the cowboys carried guns on this drive, mainly because of the threat from predatory animals and perhaps to pick off a few grouse to supplement rations on the way. The majority of them came only as far as the winter camp because only a few cowboys were needed to herd the cattle through the winter.

When spring broke and the drive was set to continue, Thaddeus Harper assessed the situation. From the Columbia River to the nearest rail transportation at Kelton, Utah, north of Salt Lake, was a drive of about six hundred miles. Shipping from there to Chicago would have cost about $250 for a car of twenty head, and prices in Chicago had plummeted. Undaunted, Harper and his cowboys pushed on, spending the summer of 1877 in Idaho. Here they held and fattened up the cattle until Harper could decide what to do with them.

Sure enough, typical of Harper's combination of business acumen and sheer luck, the story ended happily. The *British Colonist* reported the following February:

"Some eighteen months ago Mr. Thaddeus Harper drove from British Columbia into Northern Idaho 1200 head of beef cattle. These cattle were summered during 1877 in Idaho, where there was scarcity of neither water nor feed. The drought in California during the same year caused the death of many thousand head of stock, and now Mr. Harper's band is coming into market at San Francisco. The cattle are large and well-grown beeves, rolling in fat, and have been sold at $70 per head."

Harper profited enormously from this venture and, inspired by his success, made arrangements for shipping additional cattle to San Francisco. This helped to take pressure off the overstocked ranges of the BC Interior. His epic cattle drive became one of the legends in BC ranching history.

The Lillooet Trail

THE 1870S BROUGHT STRUGGLE AND despair for the fledgling British Columbia ranching industry. After the exciting years of the Cariboo gold rush and the promise of growth that came with joining the new Confederation of Canada, the economy slowed to a stop. Population growth stagnated, and markets for Interior beef were few. For the ranchers of the Cariboo, the markets of New Westminster and Victoria seemed impossibly distant. They believed the answer lay in the construction of a road from Lillooet via Pemberton Meadows to Squamish and then over the mountains to Burrard Inlet.

It took four years of political wrangling and the begrudging release of provincial funds to begin construction of the trail. It was completed to a point on Burrard Inlet between the Seymour and Lynn Rivers in October 1877. Although the road was not completed until late in the season, when snow in the high passes was already starting to accumulate, residents of the Lillooet area were eager to try it out. Among others, Richard Hooey was convinced that the trail would make Lillooet the most important city in the Interior. He had been a strong advocate of the trail and was constantly frustrated with the delays in its completion. Despite the lateness of the season, he and his partner, Robert Carson, enlisted help from a local Indigenous man, Pecullah Kosta, and decided to drive a herd of two hundred head to the coast on the new road. They set out over the rocky trail with their cattle strung out in single file and their pack horses loaded with enough food to see them to the coast. The drive to the coast was easy enough, and the trail provided sufficient feed for the cattle along the way. The trail was rocky, though adequate, and Hooey's expedition reached Squamish with their herd intact and in good health. But this had been the easy part.

The trail from Squamish to the mouth of the Seymour River on Burrard Inlet was incredibly rough, and the winter rains rendered it a sea of mud in places. The cattle suffered terribly from the constant wet, and the swollen creeks littered with numerous fallen trees made for slow going. Feed became scarce and the weary cattle lost weight rapidly. By the time they reached Burrard Inlet, the cattle were skinny and trail-worn, but not one cow had been lost in the long journey. Their view across Burrard Inlet to the smoky little settlement of Gastown offered little encouragement to the drovers. The small village showed no signs of the boom city it would become within ten years and offered no hope of a major market. A few head could be sold to the locals, but the best option was to winter the cattle and hope for a spring market.

The cattle were taken across the inlet a few at a time to the McLeery farm, on the north arm of the Fraser, where Robert Carson spent the winter feeding and caring for them. Carson sold the remaining cattle in the spring and headed back to his ranch on Pavilion Mountain, wiser but not a great deal richer. Carson and his partner's experience prompted an inquiry that concluded the trail was not fit to drive cattle over. The north section became a seldom-used route for prospectors and hunters, and the section from Pemberton to Squamish, nothing more than a pack trail for supplies to the Pemberton Valley until the railway came through in 1924. Today a modern highway connects Pemberton to Squamish via Whistler.

The "Okanagon" Post Office

LIFE ON THE FRONTIER, FAR from one's home, is always difficult. For the young men and women who came to British Columbia to settle and make a life for themselves, loneliness and homesickness were real problems. Tom Ellis, who settled at the foot of Okanagan Lake in 1865, spoke for many settlers when he wrote in his diary, "Have been alone for 10 days and am so tired of this solitude, with nothing to do. I would not mind so much if I had a good book to read." To these young people, mostly men, one of the highlights of their lives was to receive mail from home. Even the most mundane facts were important to them as they tried to keep their focus not on the day-to-day trials but on happy memories of home. But getting mail to the isolated corners of the new colony was not easy.

In the earliest days of settlement in the Okanagan Valley, when only a handful of white settlers lived in the area, mail was usually carried on horseback from Fort Kamloops or Cache Creek by anyone travelling into the Valley. By 1870, there was a post office at Kamloops and Monte Creek (Duck's and Pringle's) but, as more settlers arrived in the Okanagan, there was a growing demand for regular mail delivery. When British Columbia joined the Canadian Confederation in 1871, postal services were operated from Ottawa. It was there that the settlers of the Okanagan and Nicola districts sent a petition in March of 1872 requesting mail service for their valleys. The petition brought immediate results, reflecting perhaps the efforts of the new Dominion to please its newest member, British Columbia. On August 6, it was announced that Chief Postal Inspector Mr. Dewe had "made temporary arrangements with Mr. Barnard for a weekly mail service to Kamloops and Okanagan." To accomplish this, a new branch of the famous Barnard's Express Company stagecoach (or BX as it was universally known) was established to run on the new wagon road from Kamloops to Okanagan. This road terminated at the ranches of Cornelius O'Keefe and Thomas Greenhow, who had settled at the head of the Lake in 1867. At that time, the term "Okanagan" referred to their small settlement, and it was there that the new post office was established on August 14, 1872, called the "Okanagon" Post Office. This different spelling was probably the result of a copying error on the part of the clerk in Ottawa. Nonetheless, the name retained that spelling for the next thirty-three years when it finally was corrected to "Okanagan."

Cornelius O'Keefe was appointed the postmaster for this new office and, to accommodate the office, he built a small general store, probably the first one in the entire Okanagan Valley. Once a week, the BX stagecoach would arrive at the O'Keefe Ranch, drop off mail and passengers, and turn around and head back to Kamloops. It was not until 1876 that the wagon road was extended to points south of the O'Keefe Ranch, and not until 1887 that a post office was established in the little community of Priest's Valley, later known as Vernon.

Newman Squires:
King of the Range

NEWMAN SQUIRES WAS BORN IN Missouri in 1839 and, after the death of his parents when he was nine, traveled with relatives to California. Squires joined Jerome Harper in driving cattle from California to British Columbia during the earliest years of the gold rush. Thanks to his abilities and character, he soon took charge of the British Columbia end of the Harper drives, meeting the drive of about five hundred head of cattle at Osoyoos Lake and making sure that they arrived at the Cariboo market in good shape. During the height of the gold rush years, he oversaw three drives a year of cattle, horses, and milk cows, all destined for sale.

Squires was an expert at roping or horse breaking and always rode the finest and best-trained horses. A deadly shot with the Colt revolver, those who knew him said that it was "head or no chicken" at twenty-five paces. He was also a man of sterling character, honest and quiet about his own abilities. He never drank or used tobacco in any form and, unlike the average cowboy, was never known to use profanity of any sort. He was a big, good-looking man in his prime who was liked by everyone who knew him and was a born leader.

After the gold rush years, Squires looked after the Harper cattle interests at the Harper Ranch near Kamloops and, later, at the Gang Ranch in the Chilcotin. He was in charge of the great Harper drive from the Chilcotin in 1876 that ended up in San Francisco two years later. On this and other drives, he showed an incredible memory for the cattle in his care. After a few days on the trail, he would have all the cattle fixed in his mind. They would always be kept under night guard and counted every morning. Squires and one of his cowboys would take their places about thirty yards apart and let the stock drift through to get a correct count. If two or three had strayed off during the night, he would describe them in detail. The cowboys would shake their heads in disbelief, but sure enough, when the cattle were found, Squires' description was inevitably correct.

Squires married a Shuswap woman, Sophie. They had two children, Lucinda and Charles, and eventually purchased a ranch at Copper Creek, where Squires raised his own cattle and kept a few racehorses. Like most of the men who had been in British Columbia during the gold rush, he dabbled in mining, having an interest in several copper claims near his ranch.

Newman Squires died from heart trouble in 1898 at the age of fifty-nine. His funeral was widely attended, and his obituary was accompanied by a poem that was signed simply "D":

Hang the saddle up, tie the lariat on,
the rider's day is past and o'er;
Turn the old horse loose on the range to feed,
thro' day and night for evermore;
The snow lies light on the hill tops white,
drapes the pine trees, drapes the plains;
Nature weeps and supplies a shroud for
the old time King of Rope and Range.

*

Never again shall the untamed steed feel
the master's hand and the master know,
Never again shall the rope fly swift from the
master's hand with his one sure throw;
Never again shall the driven steer hear
the master's voice on the overland trail.
Never again shall the wild range see his form
'neath the sun or the moonlight pale.

*

Oh! Newman Squires, when the canting friars have
lost their jobs and God puts men true,
True to the best that exists in man,
to corral the sinners, He'll call on you.
Oh! Newman Squires, God speed you well,
o'er the narrow trail that all must go
At peace with God, at peace with men,
'neath the green turf sod in peace lie low.

<<< 3 >>>

Multiracial Families

OF ALL THE RANCHERS WHO settled in the Okanagan Valley in the 1860s and 1870s, a significant majority of them had Indigenous wives. They were aided by the fact that they had a common language to communicate in, as everyone spoke the Chinook jargon, the trade language of the Pacific Northwest. While these relationships would be what we now call "common law," both rancher and wife looked upon it as a permanent thing. These young women became devoted helpmates, quick to learn the running of a household. Not only did the women prove to be excellent companions for the young men, they also brought with them extended families that were willing and able to assist in the ranch activities. They adapted quickly to the ways of their husbands but maintained close contacts with their own people and culture.

The children of these liaisons formed the vast majority of children in the Valley. The first school in the Okanagan, started at Okanagan Mission (later Kelowna) in 1875, consisted entirely of the children from mixed-race marriages. The school records show that about fifteen Okanagan settlers, most of them ranchers, enrolled their children in this school, often at considerable expense to themselves. Two of its three school trustees, Frederick Brent and William Smithson, had Indigenous wives. When geologist George Mercer

Dawson passed through the Valley in 1877, he commented that "there is a school with about 20 scholars (all half-breeds) some of whom we met on the way to the mines, with lunches & books, neatly dressed."

The second school in the Okanagan Valley was opened in 1884 at Priest's Valley (later Vernon). Once again, two of the three trustees, Edward Tronson and Alfred McNeil, had mixed-race families, and almost all of the pupils were from mixed families. A teacher at the Okanagan Mission school in 1883 reported, "With one exception the pupils are half-breeds, & speak better Chinook & Indian than English & those who have a French father speak French, Indian & Chinook at home & English only at school." Two years later, residents of the Coldstream Valley formed their own school. Charles Brewer, who wrote to the provincial government to request approval, was married to an Indigenous woman, and his family, along with that of George Keefer, Stephen Lambert, and Vincent Duteau, all of whom had Indigenous wives, supplied thirteen of the fourteen school-aged pupils.

It is safe to say that mixed-race families were the norm in the early Okanagan and generally acceptable to all. But, with the coming of the railroad to British Columbia and the influx of white women, things began to change drastically. No longer were the Indigenous wives an accepted part of the community, and racial discrimination began to raise its head. These "first families" of the Okanagan Valley were looked down upon, and the children, once accepted by all, began to feel the sting of being considered inferior simply because of their parentage.

Lucy Richter

AS I'VE DESCRIBED, THE "first families" of the Okanagan Valley were composed of the union of white ranchers and Indigenous women who, along with their "mixed-race" children, formed almost the entire population of the Valley. These Indigenous wives were an important part of the ranching community and, until the arrival of "civilization," were accepted by everyone.

One such woman was Lucy, a member of the Similkameen band, who married Frank Richter. Joseph Richter, one of her five sons, remembered her contribution to the family: "When I was little, coal oil was brought 70 miles from Hope on the backs of horses. It was used sparingly. My mother made candles in a special mould and after the cotton wick was threaded, it was filled with our own tallow. She made soap from waste fat and lye. Some of our clothing was made from buckskin traded from the Indians. Mother fashioned it into coats, shirts and pants. Take it from me, buckskin garments are warm, soft and comfortable ... I suppose that today most people would think that our early days were rough. We worked hard, we had everything we needed. We were a closely knit, affectionate family, self-sufficient, yet depending on one another, each respecting the other's worth under the guidance of wise parents."

As I've noted, the Indigenous women and their children formed the majority of the population in the pre-railway days and were generally accepted by all. The children of the Indigenous women and non-Indigenous men, living far from the cities at a time when only the occasional stranger would pass by, enjoyed a life of freedom and closeness to nature that they would remember with fondness in later years. Joseph Richter reminisced about the early days: "I shall never forget those early ranch days. The valley was all ours, our lush meadows, hay fields and miles of bunchgrass range, dotted with cattle, stretched as far as we could see, to be broken here and there by snake fences. Near the house our saddle stock and milk cows grazed in the rich home pasture."

From all accounts, the marriage was a happy one, but like most, not without its ups and downs. The story is told of the time Frank Richter was struggling to cross the Similkameen River at near-flood state and began to flounder in the strong current. Lucy picked up a fence rail and extended it to him so she could pull him safely to shore. Once he regained solid ground, Lucy used the fence rail to beat him soundly for risking his life unnecessarily.

Frank Richter, probably because he was the biggest rancher in the Similkameen, stayed with his wife, Lucy, for many years. But eventually, even he succumbed to the pressure, in what we might now call a mid-life crisis, by marrying a seventeen-year-old white woman, Florence Louden, in 1894, when he was fifty-six years old. According to Louden's brother, Richard, however, Richter did not discard Lucy completely: "Immediately after his marriage to my sister, Richter established a home for Lucy and provided for her as long as she lived. She never wanted for anything ... Lucy, the Indian wife, died in about 1903 or 1904 in the cabin she lived in on the original Richter Ranch."

Mixed-race Advantages

A LIST OF THE RANCHERS who lived with Indigenous women reads like a "Who's Who" of the early ranching community. Ranchers such as J.C. Haynes, Forbes Vernon, and Cornelius O'Keefe in the Okanagan Valley, along with John Allison and Barrington Price in the nearby Similkameen, all had Indigenous wives. The same was the case in the Cariboo, where Herman Otto Bowe, founder of the Alkali Lake ranch, William Pinchbeck at Williams Lake, and Louis Antoine Minnaberriet, founder of the Basque Ranch, were all married to Indigenous women. While most of these men chose to live in a common-law relationship, there were a significant number who made their unions official with a formalized marriage.

While mixed-race families were the norm in the early British Columbia Interior, over time the children of these marriages began to feel the brunt of discrimination as "civilization" arrived in the region. Little is recorded of how these children reacted to the growing bias directed at them. But some of the children of these mixed-race families spoke and wrote of the pride they felt in growing up between two heritages.

Maria Brent, the daughter of Charles Houghton, who founded the Coldstream Ranch, and his Okanagan wife, Sophia, was keen to point out the advantages of the two heritages that she possessed. She wrote:

"they seem to possess a certain mental aloofness, a freedom and independence of judgement which makes them different from the whites, pure blood; and these qualities make for leadership among men. The half breed will either live entirely to himself, or, if he takes part in community life at all, he is apt to forge to the front. These men are in a sense 'well born.' They, on the one side of the house at least, have descended from a race of men who for many generations never knew what it was to receive a command from another and feel that they were under compulsion and bound to obey that command. Always they were free men, and, they will say, blood will tell."

To those of them who were able to articulate it, mixed-race children seemed to embody what were seen as the best qualities of both races. Eliza Swalwell observed that, "I do not know whether this responsiveness to certain beautiful aspects of nature comes to me from my Indian mother or from my father's side. It seems to me the whites are too much bound and limited, too enslaved by their written creeds and confessions of faith ... Standing as I do between the two races I could never see that intellectually the Indians are not the equals of the whites. The Indians are sadly lacking in culture; that is to be seen at a glance, but social grace and refinement are things which can be acquired ... Why should any man, whether Indian or white, be commiserated because he sees in the workings of nature manifestations of the Creator? He would be a dolt if he did not."

Maria Houghton Brent

MARIA BRENT WAS A PASSIONATE advocate of the mixed-race children of the early Okanagan ranchers and their Indigenous wives that formed the "first families" of the Valley. She once wrote, "This is an aspect of Canadian history which seems to have been strangely overlooked, viz., the natural aptitude of men of mixed Indian and white blood, for public office and for leadership."

Her father, Charles Frederick Houghton, was born in Ireland and entered the British Army at the age of sixteen. After serving eight years, he heard that the colonial government was offering land grants of 1440 acres to military settlers with the rank of Captain. When he travelled to British Columbia he was told that the land grants had been reduced. Nonetheless he took up land in the Okanagan Valley along with his friends, the brothers Forbes and Charles Vernon, after whom the City of Vernon is named. He appealed to the government of the Colony of British Columbia for a full military grant and received a total of 1450 acres, which he named the Coldstream Ranch.

In 1868 or 1969, Houghton met and married Sophie N'kwala, granddaughter of the great Okanagan Chief N'kwala. It was Chief N'kwala who personally conducted the wedding ceremony, indicating the significance and permanence of the union. The couple had two children; Maria was born in 1870 and baptised at Okanagan Mission (later Kelowna). Her brother Edward was born in 1872. The happy family did not survive for long. In 1877, in the altogether too common practice in the BC Interior, the 39 year-old Charles Houghton married 22 year-old Marion Dunsmuir, daughter of the well-to-do coal magnate, Robert Dunsmuir. His wife Sophie and the children returned to their Okanagan Indigenous relatives.

Maria Houghton was a strong, intelligent young woman and this was recognized by her Okanagan family. As she later wrote, "In an Indian tribe they pick one sober child with a good memory and train them to remember the story of their family and their ancestors. I was chosen for this. It was my great grandfather's daughter that taught me (my grand aunt, old N'kwala's daughter, young N'kwala's sister). I now lived with my grandfather's sister." Maria's great aunt taught her the traditions, which she had learned from her father, the old Chief N'kwala. Maria, who had been well schooled, wrote down these traditions, preserving them for future generations.

When Charles Houghton's wife Marion died in 1893, he invited Maria to Montreal, where he was stationed. She attended the balls and social events of the Montreal upper class and enjoyed a glimpse of how the other half lived. Her father retired to Victoria in 1897 and passed away the following year. Maria returned to her Okanagan family, quite a contrast from the life in Montreal. She married William Brent, mixed-race son of Okanagan pioneer Frederick Brent and his wife Mary Ann, a daughter of Chief N'kwala. Maria Brent became widely known in the North Okanagan Valley and was the author of a number of historical articles in the Okanagan Historical Society reports.

Eliza Jane Swalwell

IN THIS CHAPTER, I HAVE been looking at the Okanagan Valley's "first families," the marriages of white settlers with Indigenous women and their mixed-race families. One of these families was the Swalwells. George Simpson was born in Philadelphia of Scottish Presbyterian parents and married an Indigenous Okanagan woman. Their daughter, Eliza Jane Swalwell, looked back at her childhood in an account of her "Girlhood Days in the Okanagan." "I remember this valley when everything was in a wild state, before there was any wagon road and everything had to be brought in by pack-train, and all our dishes were of tin, and we baked bread and pies and roasted meat in a Dutch oven.

To those children of mixed-race families, there was no feeling that they were in some way different. In fact, the vast majority of families in the

Okanagan were of this type. The Valley was cattle country in those days of the 1870s and first half of the 1880s and lay unfenced from one end to the other. Eliza recalled the beauty of the Valley: "To me it was an exquisite pleasure as a girl to ride over this green and gracious pasture land in the mornings, and to see it stretching before me for miles with the Sand Rose lying scattered on the ground as if a fairy princess had passed that way at dawn and children had strewn flowers in her path, and to see the sunlight on the hills. On such occasions I have sometimes seen things, or rather sensed something, so serene and beautiful that it left me weak and weeping as I sat in the saddle."

Life was not all fun, though. All the children in these families pitched in to help with the ranch work, and girls were not exempt: "Before the arrival of the wagon road everyone had to learn to ride, as it was the only means of getting anywhere, and we girls were all proficient horsewomen. We could round up a band of horses, drive them into a corral, rope the one we wanted and saddle him up as expertly as a man could do it ... The two great events of the year were the coming of the cattle buyers in May and September. They usually sent word ahead to let us know they were coming, and then we all got busy, and everyone, girls as well as men, assisted in the round-up. On these occasions we girls felt that we were coming into our own. We could handle a horse about as well as the men, and we could show them that we amounted to something more than a mere nuisance about the place, as they sometimes seemed to think we were."

Discrimination

WE HAVE SEEN IN PREVIOUS columns that the "first families" of the Okanagan consisted of a white rancher and his Okanagan wife with their mixed-race children. Throughout the early years of settlement in the 1860s, 1870s, and early 1880s, these families were in the majority and considered perfectly normal. But as the interior of British Columbia opened up to more and more settlers, couples in mixed-race relationships began to find themselves in the minority and subject to discrimination. White men who had not formalized their relationship through marriage, especially those who had arrived early in the Interior and were owners of extensive lands and "pillars of the community," were pressured to discard their Indigenous wives. This ugly discrimination that newcomers directed against men with Indigenous wives (referred to sneeringly as "klootch," for the Chinook word for "woman") is typified in the reminiscences of Sydney Russell Almond, recorded some years later, which reveals a disappointingly common attitude. He says of early Similkameen rancher Barrington Price: "He came of a good family in England and evidently had rich connections ... He married a klootch and wrote home to his friends that he had married an Indian princess. I don't know what idea his friends had of an Indian princess as they come in British Columbia, but it is safe to say that they had no such picture of her as the actual Indian klootch as we know here, even when married to a self-respecting white man."

Time did not lessen the discrimination, and it seeped into the public domain as well. Henry Bigby Shuttleworth, the son of a major English landowner, Lord Shuttleworth, had married an Indigenous woman when he arrived in the Similkameen in the 1870s. Some years later, he was looking for a teaching position and, after being turned down for several openings, wrote, "I suppose it is because I have an Indian Woman but I can assure you and if necessary prove to you that I am lawfully married to her."

Inevitably, as more and more white women arrived in the area, the pressure became overwhelming and led at best to a discreet hiding of the Indigenous woman and her children. Edward Tronson owned the Vernon Hotel and experienced much discrimination by newcomers over Nancy, his wife of many years, and their six children. He is described in *Valley of Youth*, written by C.W. Holiday, who came to the Okanagan in the 1880s, as a "courtly-groomed old gentleman. But to see him in church looking rather like a saintly old patriarch you would never have suspected that on his ranch he maintained an Indian wife and a large half-breed family; a quite separate establishment, none of them ever appeared in public with him." More commonly, the Indigenous wife was rejected and sent back to her people, leaving the rancher to feel free to remarry a white woman.

This sad story of the rejection of the Indigenous wives by the early ranchers was repeated all through the British Columbia Interior. For a time, the story of these "first families" of the Interior was largely ignored in most of the histories of the area. But, in more recent times, the stories of these founding families are finally being told.

<<< **4** >>>

Cowboy Culture

Buckaroos

ALTHOUGH CATTLE HAD BEEN DOMESTICATED for thousands of years, it was in southern Spain that cattle herders first worked on horseback. The mounted herdsmen, called *vaqueros*, or "cow herders," were the first in what was to be a long line of men on horseback who tended to the cattle of the rich landowners. They were a rough lot, these *vaqueros*, living on the fringes of civilization and not always viewed favourably by their more conventional neighbours. And yet, many civilized folk regarded them with a certain amount of envy for their carefree existence.

From their origins in southern Spain, the techniques and lifestyle of the *vaquero* spread to the New World, first to the islands of the Caribbean and then to the mainland of Mexico. From there the *vaqueros* travelled to California and up the west coast of America. In the process, the Spanish term *"vaquero"* became anglicized to "buckaroo."

The *vaquero* or buckaroo was distinctive from his counterpart east of the Rockies. He used a long braided rawhide rope, called *la reata* or, as it became in English, lariat. This type of rope was extremely long, usually sixty feet, allowing the *vaquero* to rope a steer at a great distance. But the lariat did not lend itself to being tied to the saddle horn like the grass ropes east of the Rockies. So the *vaquero* wrapped his rope a few turns around the saddle horn, as he termed it, *dar la veulta* or "to take a turn." Needless to say, the English-speaking buckaroos had trouble with pronouncing this and came up with the term "dally." A dally roper was one who preferred to wrap his rope around the saddle horn rather than tie it "hard and fast." Since the impact on the saddle using the dally technique was that much less, the *vaquero* only used one cinch to hold his saddle onto the horse, unlike the cowboys on the other side of the mountains, who tied hard and fast and used doubled-cinched saddles.

The buckaroo was also distinctive in how he dressed and how he equipped his horse. As with his Spanish-speaking predecessor, the buckaroo liked lots of silver, using *conchos* (from Spanish "shells") on his hat and on his rigging. He also preferred to use a wide, flat-brimmed hat similar to the Spanish *sombrero* to shield his face and eyes from the hot sun.

As the cattle that were driven into British Columbia in the gold rush days came mostly from Oregon, it is not surprising that among the first drovers, the buckaroo influence predominated. Braided rawhide ropes and single-cinched "Mexican" saddles were prevalent. Over the years, as cowboys travelled back and forth across the Rocky Mountains, the distinct dress and gear of the buckaroo began to be mixed with the that of the cowboys east of the mountains. But, even to this day, the term "buckaroo" refers to the men who handle cattle west of the Rocky Mountains, especially in the Great Basin area of Utah, Nevada, and Oregon. And the *vaquero* influence can still be seen in British Columbia.

The Chinook Language

EARLY BRITISH COLUMBIA COWBOYS WERE allegedly masters of three languages: English, Chinook, and profane. It is no exaggeration to say that, west of the Rocky Mountains, throughout the Pacific Northwest, the common language spoken by the Indigenous people and the early settlers was Chinook. It was a language that consisted of a mixture of Indigenous dialects, French, and English.

Long before European contact, the Indigenous people of the northwest spoke dozens of distinct and unique languages. In the area of present-day British Columbia, there were at least thirty languages, not including different dialects within the languages. Indigenous People had traded for countless centuries before the explorers and fur traders arrived, and it was not unusual to find seashells and oolichan grease (rendered from a small fish) far inland from the coastal areas where they were obtained. Trading is always easier when buyer and seller share a common language, and so a language of trade, comprising the simplest terms of expression, evolved. The earliest fur traders adapted and added to that common language. The French "joual" of the Quebecois and Metis fur traders, the English of the Yorkshiremen, and the Gaelic of the Scots found their way into the mix. When the earliest missionaries, settlers, and drovers arrived, they encountered a complete language that could be spoken to Indigenous people or newcomers anywhere in British Columbia. Even though its grammar and vocabulary were limited, the new language displayed a flexibility and power of expression that met every need of normal conversation.

Many of the earliest cowboys were of Indigenous or mixed-blood origin so it was only natural that Chinook become the most commonly spoken language of the ranches in the Interior. It remained the main form of communication between the Indigenous People and whites until well after 1900. As one early settler observed, "In those early days we in British Columbia, were more or less a bilingual race. The Custom's Officer on the wharf at New Westminster, pointing to some baggage, would say to some newly-arrived immigrant just off the boat from San Francisco, 'Are these your "*iktas*"?' (things), and the schoolboys at play would shout, '*Klosh nanitch,*' instead of 'Look out.' The children did not go to school to learn Chinook, they grew up with it."

Some common words for the cowboy speaker of Chinook included:

kiuatan—horse
moosmoos—cattle, buffalo
klootchman moosmoos—cow
kamooks—dog
lemel—mule
callipeen—rifle/musket
lope—rope
lewhet—whip
seapo—hat
siskiyou—a bobtailed horse
kishkish—to drive
tupso—grass
lamonti—mountain
stick shoes—boots

A basic understanding of Chinook allowed a person of any race or language to understand such a command as "Mamook kishkish moosmoos kah cole chako"; everyone in his party, whether Indigenous, European, or, for that matter Chinese, would know he meant "Drive the cattle north." The Chinook jargon provided the First Peoples of British Columbia a distinct advantage over their prairie counterparts because there was no language barrier to hamper their ability to understand simple directions. This may account for the large number of Indigenous cowboys in British Columbia during the earliest days of the cattle industry, something that continues to this day.

Today the Chinook dialect survives in British Columbia in place names such as Skookumchuk (Chinook *skookum* = strong, *chuck* = water) for "rapids" or *Canim* (canoe) Lake, and in regular vocabulary such as *skookum* (strong, brave), *mowitch* (deer), or *saltchuck* (*salt* = sea, *chuck* = water). But the spoken language has long since disappeared from common usage.

British Columbia's Indigenous Cowboys

THE LATE SUMMER DAY WAS hot and dry. The herd of cattle crossed the line into the new Crown Colony of British Columbia raising clouds of choking dust for those who drove them. The year was 1861. The cattle, owned by Major John Thorpe, were being driven to the goldfields of the Cariboo country to feed the thousands of miners that were flocking to the area. Through the dust could be seen the drovers (the term "cowboy" had not come into use yet) who were working for Thorpe. The crew consisted of young Jack Splawn and Joe Evans; a mixed-race man named Paul; and Indigenous members Cultus John, Ken-e-ho, and Ken-e-ho's wife, who also drove cattle and cooked for the crew. What is remarkable is not the fact that about half the party were Indigenous, but that this proportion of Indigenous drovers was normal. Indigenous People were a significant part of the labour force on the early cattle drives. A similar party led by Myron Brown in 1868 consisted of five whites and five Indigenous People, "with all a rather agreeable crowd all things considered," as Brown recorded. During the years 1858 to 1868, over ten thousand head of cattle were driven over the trails of British Columbia to the goldfields, and Indigenous drovers were on most of the drives.

In British Columbia, Indigenous cowboys were the backbone of ranch labour from the very beginning, but in Alberta and Saskatchewan, they were slow to be accepted by the industry. Why was this so? What factors in British Columbia made the Indigenous cowboy such an integral part of the early ranching industry when the same was not the case east of the Rockies?

The use of Chinook in bridging the language barrier was the most important factor in the acceptance of the Indigenous men as drovers. The ability to communicate has the effect of breaking down many of the prejudices that so often divide the races. Adding to the acceptance that came from easy communication was the sometimes grudging admission that the Indigenous cowboys were superb horsemen.

This acceptance found another form in the predominantly male frontier. As I've described, many of the earliest ranchers in British Columbia married

Indigenous women, and the children of these mixed-race marriages worked on the ranches of the Interior. These children were among the best working cowboys in British Columbia as the ranching industry grew and prospered on the bunchgrass ranges of the Interior.

Throughout ranching country, Indigenous and mixed-blood cowboys worked alongside young men from all over the world and, most often, the Indigenous cowboys were the acknowledged experts. Working cowboys like Antoine Allen, who came north with the Harper Brothers in the 1860s and was still driving cattle in 1913, or Okanagan Native Joseph George (Susap), who cowboyed and packed for ranches in the South Okanagan, were acknowledged as the best of their kind. Many Indigenous and mixed-blood cowboys rose to be leaders in the ranching community. This was the case with Joe Coutlee, who was cow boss of the Douglas Lake Ranch for forty-eight years. The same qualities could be found in the early rodeo world, where horse contractor Hans Richter was acknowledged as one of the best pickup men in early rodeo. His lead was followed by Louis Bates and Gus Gottfriedson, who became horse contractors in the 1940s and 1950s, and rodeo cowboys like Dave Perry and Louie Bates, who excelled in the rough world of rodeo. Their tradition of excellence has continued in such modern-day heroes as Kenny McLean, the great bronc rider. Even today, a visit to the cow camps and big ranches of the British Columbia Interior will show that Indigenous cowboys are still a vital part of the ranching community.

Susap

SOME OF THE BEST COWBOYS in British Columbia have been Okanagan Indigenous People. Their knowledge of the land and their incredible skill with horses has long been recognized. One of the earliest and most remarkable was Susap, who was a member of the Nk'mip (Inkameep) band.

Eneas Susap, who was also called Eneas Joe and Yankin, was an Okanagan man who was well known throughout the South Okanagan and

Similkameen as a cowboy and packer. He was one of three brothers who made their mark in the region as honourable, honest men and excellent stockmen. One of his brothers, Baptiste, became Chief of the Nk'mip band in 1907.

Susap went to work for Barrington Price in the Keremeos area in 1872 and rapidly gained a reputation as an accomplished horseman and diligent worker. Before long, John Carmichael Haynes asked him to come work for him at his ranch near Osoyoos Lake. Susap took over the care and training of Haynes's large herd of horses. He was an outstanding rider and could handle and break the most difficult of horses.

Susap soon proved himself indispensable to the Haynes family. When the Haynes house caught fire in 1878, it was Susap who rushed into the burning house and carried the Haynes children, Hester and Val, to safety. A few years later, he was out on Osoyoos Lake with two of the Haynes children when he saw little Will Haynes fall into the lake and disappear under the surface. Susap dove into the lake, swam to the drowning child, and pulled him out of the water. He tipped the boy upside down to let water pour out of his boots and mouth, then ran with him to the house, where he revived him and wrapped him in a warm blanket. The Haynes family expressed their gratitude by giving Susap a new outfit of clothes and boots every Christmas.

Susap's skills with horses made him an excellent packer, and he was regularly entrusted with taking a pack train to Hope and back over the Dewdney Trail for supplies for the Haynes family and other South Okanagan and Similkameen ranchers. In 1880, after taking cattle to Hope over the Dewdney Trail, he became the guide and packer for Bishop and Mrs. A.W. Sillitoe from Hope to Osoyoos over the trail. The trip is recorded in Mrs. Sillitoe's diary, and she mentions Susap's ability to weave a bed of cedar boughs, "in the spreading of which the Indians are adepts. If skilfully laid, they form a very easy, springy bed, but woe betide the unfortunate traveller who tries to sleep on a brush bed not scientifically spread." Susap, for some time afterward, was referred to as "Sillitoe" in memory of his services to the Bishop.

When J.C. Haynes died in 1888, Susap went to work for other ranches in the South Okanagan. He married Sophie and had two children, Manuel and Margaret. Susap lived to be 106 years old and was esteemed by both Indigenous People and whites as one of the best horsemen and honest workers in the area.

Pack Trains into the Wilderness

DURING THE GOLD RUSH DAYS of the 1860s, prospectors penetrated deep into the rugged wilderness in the BC Interior, carrying all their supplies on their backs. When a discovery was made, a little mining town would spring up, consisting of a series of shacks strung out along a creek. These towns were connected to the outside world by narrow trails over extremely rough country. So the challenge was always to somehow transport enough goods to these towns to feed, clothe, and supply the miners. The only way to do this was through pack trains.

The earliest packers in British Columbia came from Mexico. Many of these had been involved in the California gold rush and had drifted north as the mining frontier advanced. They brought with them the equipment and techniques that had been developed in the mountains of Mexico many years before. Not surprisingly, most of the terminology of early packing was Spanish. The boss of the pack train, consisting of about thirty to a hundred loaded animals, was the *cargadero,* and the *arrieros* were the men who did the packing. The lead animal was the *mulara,* and the whole train the *caballada.* These pack trains penetrated deep into the heart of the wilderness, bringing supplies to the isolated communities of the province.

The key to successful packing was to keep the backs of the pack horses or mules (the preferred pack animal) from developing sores from the heavy loads. To this end, the *aparejo* (ap-a-ray-ho) was used. It consisted of two long leather sacks joined in the middle and stuffed with straw. The *aparejo* was placed on top of three different cloths, so that the animal's back was carefully padded and tightly cinched down. On top of the *aparejo*, which extended down either side of the animal's back, were piled the goods to be packed, averaging three hundred pounds per animal.

The greatest of all BC packers was Jean Caux, known to all as "Cataline" because he was mistakenly believed to come from Catalonia in Spain. Caux actually came from France and arrived in BC in the early years of the Cariboo gold rush. He soon established a reputation of being able to deliver his pack trains to the most remote, inaccessible locations, which he did continuously for the next fifty years. Cataline was a colourful character. His thick black hair reached to his shoulders, and his usual headgear was a sombrero. He wore heavy woollen trousers, riding boots (that concealed a deadly Mexican knife), a silk scarf around his neck, and a stiffly starched shirt that started out each trip new and was discarded when the trip was successfully completed. In all his years packing into the rugged Interior, Cataline never failed to deliver his cargo on time. He was a friend to the Indigenous people and always donned a high French hat and ancient frock coat to trade with them. His preferred drink was cognac, but he would settle for brandy. Whatever the beverage, it was his habit, after each drink, to take a small amount of alcohol and rub it into his hair, saying in his thick accent, "A little insida, a little outsida."

<<< **5** >>>

Tools of the Trade

Saddles

THE FIRST SADDLES TO ARRIVE in North America were primarily Spanish war saddles with high cantles, to keep the rider from being driven over the back of his horse, and high forks to protect the rider in front. Once the Spanish established their dominance over the Indigenous people of Central America, their attention shifted to development of the resources in the new land, and the raising of cattle became a major industry. The Mexican *vaqueros* found that the war saddle was not suited for working cattle in the wide-open spaces of Mexico. They therefore developed a lighter saddle consisting only of a hide-covered tree with a rather low cantle and a short fork with no saddle horn. When a cow was roped, it was secured to the horse's tail. Not surprisingly, this was not entirely satisfactory and, by 1830, Mexican *vaqueros* had developed a saddle with a saddle horn on which to attach a rope. Thus originated the stock saddle in North America.

The early stock saddles were covered with a removable leather sheet called a *mochila*, which had slits cut in it through which the cantle and fork of the saddle protruded. Californian saddles tended to have a small horn with a small flat cap, while the Texas saddles, especially what was called the Hope Saddle, had large, flat horn caps. This difference arose because the roping techniques of the California *vaqueros* differed from their Texas counterparts. The *Californios* wrapped their braided rawhide *reatas* around the saddle horn, allowing the roper to vary the tension on the rope and save wear and tear on the saddle. The Texas cowboys preferred to tie their ropes to the saddle horn, and the resulting shock of a 1,500-pound bull hitting the end of their rope required a much thicker, sturdier horn. For the same reason, saddles in Texas were heavier and had two cinches to secure them to the horse. California saddles were lighter and single-cinched, and tended to be more ornate than their Texas cousins, with carved leather and metal *conchos*.

It was this California-style saddle that found its way north to the valleys of western Oregon and eventually to British Columbia during the gold rush years. For the British, being used to their own style of saddle, this strange aberration was a "Mexican saddle." Whatever its local name, the California stock saddle was everywhere and was used by drovers and miners alike. Photographs of the main street of Barkerville in the 1860s show the widespread use of the California saddle with the characteristic saddle horn and cantle. Most have saddle horns that are wrapped with leather around the neck but with uncovered caps; some of the saddles have *tapaderos* over the stirrups; and all appear to be "centre fire"-rigged, having a single cinch located midway on the saddle.

When the cattle industry became fully established in the British Columbia Interior, the California saddle was enthusiastically accepted as the best stock saddle by the cowboys. For years, a BC cowboy could be distinguished from his Alberta counterpart by his saddle until, as cowboys drifted back and forth across the Great Divide of the Rockies, saddle styles merged into one.

Leg Armour

SPANISH INFLUENCE PERVADES THE VOCABULARY of the cowboy, so it is not surprising to learn that the word "chaps" (pronounced "shaps") comes from the Spanish *chaparreras* meaning "leg armour." Originally a part of the saddle, they were called *armas* and came with the *vaquero* to California where they were adapted to fit over the legs.

The California *armas* eventually came to be called *chaparreras,* and were quickly adopted by the English-speaking cowboys of California. From there they spread with the Spanish cattle into Oregon, where they proved very useful in the sagebrush country of Oregon's interior. Their name was soon shortened to "chaps," and some of the early drovers into British Columbia wore them for protection from the brush and thorns found along the narrow trails.

The earliest chaps in British Columbia were a closed-leg chap consisting of two long tubes of leather into which the legs were stuck and joined into a belt at the waist. The seam was sewn on the outside of each leg with enough leather left to be cut into a fringe, an adaptation that seems to have been borrowed from the Indigenous legging. The way the two legs tapered down to the ankle reminded the drovers of the two barrels of a shotgun with a choke at the muzzle, so they called them "shotgun chaps."

Shotgun chaps were light, warm and somewhat water-resistant. But the cowboys found that oiling the chaps to make them more waterproof also made them stiff and uncomfortable in cold weather, so they started covering them with pelts of various kinds to provide more warmth in cold weather and more water resistance. Soon the chaps themselves were made of the pelts from bear, goat, deer, and other animals, with the hair left on the outside. These "woollies," as they were called, became very popular in the harsh northern climate of British Columbia. They also offered protection from bruises when a rider was thrown against a fence or tree by a mean horse. By the turn of the century, cowboys in British Columbia almost universally wore "woollies," most often made from long, thick-haired Angora goatskins.

The main drawback to shotgun chaps and woollies was the difficulty in getting them on and off. Since they were tight to the leg, they had to be pulled on over stockinged feet before the boots and spurs were put on. This was awkward and time consuming. Soon chaps were developed that buckled over the legs with snaps so the cowboy could simply fasten the belt and then reach down and snap the legs in place. This design allowed for a flap of leather to extend beyond the side of the legs, much like wings hanging back from the legs. As this flap became more pronounced, the particular style came to be known as "batwing" chaps. The plain leather surface could be decorated with silver *conchos* and leather tooling or overlays, making for a very fancy design.

The earliest chaps buckled at the back and were laced together at the front. The straight belt with a full lace front proved dangerous if a rider was pitched forward on the saddle horn. If he was hung up, it was very difficult to extract himself. Over the years, the lacing at the front became less and less, and chaps were designed with a distinct dip in the front centre. In more recent times, the two sides of the chap were joined by a single thin lace, which would break easily if the rider was hung up.

Cowboy Boots

FROM THE DAYS OF THE Mongols, who swept through eastern Europe on horseback wearing boots with high, red wooden heels, horsemen have preferred a high leather boot with an elevated heel that allowed them to place their foot securely in the stirrup. In fact, in European society of the 1600s, the distinctive riding boot became a sign of nobility. Owning and caring for a horse required significant wealth and placed a person above the common man, so riders with high heels and knee-high leather boots became associated with the upper class. To this day, we refer to someone who is wealthy or aristocratic as "well heeled."

The upper-class English who immigrated to the American South brought with them the high-heeled leather boots that indicated their class. By the early 1800s, the boots, which were shortened to just cover the calf, were named in honour of Arthur Wellesley, First Duke of Wellington, the victor at the Battle of Waterloo in 1815. During the American Civil War, all military officers and cavalry wore a "Full Wellington," a two-piece leather boot. After the war, the tens of thousands of surplus boots were sold to horsemen, especially in the West, and the Wellington became the standard boot for all western horsemen. The Coffeyville pattern, as it was called, had a higher Cuban heel than the regular military version and was favoured by the early drovers, who preferred a heel that they could brace against the stirrup when holding a taut rope. These boots travelled to British Columbia during the gold rush years with the drovers and the California miners and soon became the standard footwear.

In the late 1870s, a bootmaker named H.J. Justin of Spanish Fort, on the Red River in north Texas, modified the Full Wellington on the advice of the trail drivers to produce more of a pointed-toe boot that could be easily inserted into the stirrup. He also inserted a steel-shank arch for more riding support. The popularity of this modified boot spread rapidly throughout the West and arrived in British Columbia by the 1880s. By that time, the cowboy boot had become a separate style, with elaborate stitch patterns on the sides for more support and stovepipe tops.

The high heel remained popular on the cowboy boot because it prevented the foot from going through the stirrup and catching in such a way that the rider could be dragged by a runaway horse. Early cowboys always "homed" their foot in the stirrup, with the boots far enough into the stirrup to have the boot heels resting against the stirrup. They maintained that it was less tiring to ride this way, but it was also more difficult to extract the boot in times of trouble. The high-heeled boot was also good for digging in when the cowboy was roping on foot. The practical value of a high heel is certainly significant, but the added height that it gave to the cowboy should not be discounted. In some ways, the cowboys were not much different from the Mongols and the cavaliers.

Clothing

THE MOST DISTINCTIVE ARTICLES OF cowboy apparel were wide-brimmed hats, high-heeled boots, and leather or woolly chaps. All of these were designed for a purpose and, as is often the case with what we wear, they made a fashion statement as well. But there were many other articles of clothing that were standard for cowboys. Some were chosen for their serviceability and differed little from the clothing worn by most farm labourers of the time. We can get a glimpse of the working cowboy attire at the turn of the twentieth century in a letter written to a young Englishman, Brian Kesteven de Peyster Chance, from a former Douglas Lake Ranch cowboy, Frank Newstand. Chance was heading to British Columbia to work on the Douglas Lake Ranch and had asked Newstand for his advice on a number of matters, including what clothing to wear, to which Newstand replied:

> Now as to clothing, in the summer blue jean overalls purchased at one dollar and a quarter at the Ranche store with a cotton shirt will fill the bill; but for autumn and winter, let me most strongly recommend the best quality and warmest underclothes, vest and drawers. I found layers invaluable then good flannel shirts with ditto collars. Old fashioned velvet corduroy breeches or I prefer trousers made fairly to fit from the knees down as riding boots are distinctly cold in winter and if you get a job riding you will try a pair of chaps, and these will pull over tight trousers and you can wear either riding boots or what I prefer to ride in during zero weather, ordinary walking boots and overshoes over them ... Have a good coat and waistcoat of whipcord for winter and for the rest all the old clothes you have by you. Remember, decent underclothing, flannel shirts and boots cannot be bought in Canada, most other things are obtainable ... I think a small strong trunk with a good lock the best thing for your kit; things might be stolen from a kit-bag; if riding, one is often away from the bunk house for a week.

Newstand went on to mention that "there are plenty of good fellows in a Douglas Lake haying gang that will help a fellow along if he wants help but don't begin to tell them 'how they do things in England.' This is fatal." The young Chance must have heeded Newstand's advice well—he remained at the Douglas Lake Ranch for the next forty-two years and was manager from 1940 until 1967.

Because of the inevitable wear and tear that cowboy clothing was subjected to, everything was made of the best material and therefore cost more than the average price for clothing. Pure wool and cotton were the order of the day, and clothing was purchased large to allow for freedom of action. Pant legs were wide and long to allow the pants to ride up easily when a cowboy was in the saddle, which was most of the time. Levi Strauss denim jeans were popular throughout the ranching country as were heavy duck-canvas pants. Cotton shirts in the summer and plaid wool shirts in the winter were standard wear and, since early shirts did not come with pockets, a vest was generally worn, both for extra warmth and to supply pockets for the cowboy's "makins" (tobacco and papers) and personal items. In the summertime in British Columbia, cowboys always carried a rain slicker, made large enough to cover the entire body and legs and open up the back to fit over the horse and saddle.

Gloves, too, were standard wear for the working cowboys of British Columbia, especially when working in the brush or when dallying their ropes. Gauntlet gloves were especially popular, and the Indigenous cowboys proudly wore beautifully beaded gauntlets made by their mothers or wives. If they did not have gauntlets to cover their wrists, cowboys wore leather cuffs that laced or buckled up over their wrists. Leather cuffs usually had ornate stamping on them, purely for decorative purposes, reflecting the cowboys' surprisingly unmacho attitude that pretty worked every bit as well as plain.

This attitude of combining utility and appearance was particularly evident when it came to neck coverings. Cowboys wore neckerchiefs around their necks to pull up over the mouth when following cattle over dusty trails. Neckerchiefs were also used for warmth in the winter months and, in the coldest weather, could be tied around a rider's head to protect his ears from freezing. Silk proved to be the most effective for neckerchiefs because it kept the dust out more effectively than cotton and it kept the heat in during the winter. The cowboy's "glad rag," as the neckerchief was affectionately called, was an indispensable part of his attire.

Given the pragmatism of the cowboy's clothes, it perhaps not surprising that the cowboy style of dress has changed very little from the earliest days of the open range. Today's cowboy could easily be mistaken for his counterpart of a hundred years ago, proving that the tried-and-true clothing and gear will always be a part of cowboy tradition.

Dally Roping

A ROPE MAY LOOK LIKE a simple thing but, next to a horse, it was the most important tool of the early cowboy and continues to be an indispensable part of the cattle trade. Roping has always been the only way to catch and hold cattle and horses and the only way to throw an animal for branding or doctoring. In the hands of a competent cowboy, roping can be a skill that borders on art; it was the most difficult of all cowboy skills, and an expert roper spent most of his working life practising and perfecting his technique.

The braided rawhide rope, referred to as *la reata*, came to Mexico from the south of Spain with the first Spanish-speaking *vaqueros*. From Mexico, the use of the rope spread to California, where it became one of the most important tools for handling cattle from horseback. From there, the use of the braided rawhide rope travelled to British Columbia with the Mexican packers and other cowboys. Its Spanish name, *la reata*, soon became anglicized as "lariat."

In the hands of a Mexican *vaquero*, it was a formidable tool. As a rawhide rope is too stiff to tie hard and fast to a saddle horn and does not stand up well against the weight of a roped steer, the *vaqueros* used the technique of wrapping the rope around the saddle horn. The Spanish term "*dar la vuelta,*" meaning literally "to give it the turn" or to "give a twist" became corrupted by the English-speaking cowboys to "dally-welta" or just plain "dally." One of the true distinctions of the cowboys west of the Rocky Mountains was their technique of dallying the rope as opposed to cowboys east of the Rockies who preferred to tie their ropes to the saddle horn. Dallying a rope is easier on the stock being roped and on the saddle horse, as it eliminates the sudden jerk on the rope when the animal reaches the end of the rope. As well, in the case of an accident, the dallied rope is easier to slip off the horn.

The braided rawhide *reata* continued to be used in British Columbia until late in the 1800s. But, because there were very few good *reata* braiders, it was soon replaced with a twisted rope of manila, which soon became the fibre rope of choice among the cowboys of the West. This type of rope was cheaper and easier to make and, if well made, was stronger and had a smoother running surface. The manila hemp rope tended to be much shorter in length, averaging about forty feet in length.

Until a manila rope is limbered up, it will neither throw nor coil well. Most cowboys stretched their ropes to remove the kinks and render them pliable. Sometimes the cowboy would stretch it between two trees or fence posts. Another popular technique was for two cowboys to tie their new ropes to each other's saddle horns and back their horses up slowly to stretch their ropes. Once stretched, ropes were often conditioned with tallow or soaked in linseed oil to waterproof them and to keep them pliable. Some cowboys, however, found this made a rope too greasy to handle, and preferred to leave their rope untouched. When a rope became limp and lifeless from hard use, it was discarded and a new rope either cut from the roll at the ranch or purchased from the nearest supplier.

From Bull Whips to Quirts

ALTHOUGH THE SPANISH *vaquero* brought most of the tools of the cattle trade to the grasslands west of the Rocky Mountains, there were some items that found their origins not in the salt marshes of southwestern Spain but in the highlands of Great Britain. In Britain, the cattle herders, mostly old men and children on foot, controlled their cattle with long whips called "bullwhips." These whips were braided out of rawhide or tanned leather, and it was claimed that a good bullwhip-wielding man could control a hundred head of cattle. It is important to note that cattle were seldom struck by the whips but were controlled by the sound of the cracking of the whip beside their heads.

It is not surprising that the introduction of British breeds of cattle into Jamaica and later South Carolina in the late 1600s saw the use of the cattle whip as the main cattle-control device. In fact, the widespread use of the bullwhip gave the cowboys of the Carolinas and Florida their distinctive name "crackers," after the sound of the bullwhip that was used to manage cattle. The "crackers" became expert whip users and, on the cattle trails and grasslands of the east, the whip became the main tool of the cowboy.

The spread of cattle into the Midwest and eventually over the Oregon Trail to the area west of the Rockies also introduced the bullwhip, which proved to be indispensable in the tighter confines of the wooded valleys of Oregon and Washington. Many drovers who pushed cattle into British Columbia in the 1860s were from families who had come from the Midwest over the Oregon Trail, and they were familiar with the use of the bullwhip. One of these was Myron Brown, who was involved in three cattle drives from Oregon to British Columbia in 1867 and 1868, and in his diary frequently records "mending my whip" or "braiding a new whip," indicating how useful the bullwhip was in driving cattle.

The other type of whip used by the British Columbia cowboys was the quirt, a short flexible woven-leather whip. It was made with a handle about a foot long, and two to four heavy loose lashes hanging from one end, and the other end with a loop to hang around the cowboy's wrist or saddle horn. The word is derived from the Spanish *cuarta de cordon* meaning "whip of cord." Unlike the bullwhip, this type of whip was brought north from Mexico. The flexible handles of most quirts were loaded with shot or lead to give them weight. Some quirts were made with stiff handles because they were easier to handle. The quirt was used to strike down rearing horses that threatened to fall backward or to make a horse increase its speed.

Use of the bullwhip fell out of favour among the cowboys of British Columbia, who preferred to use the rope for controlling cattle. But anyone who has watched the classic Australian movie *The Man From Snowy River*, where the hero, Jim Craig, drives a herd of wild horses with a stock whip alone, will realize that the British practice of using a bullwhip to control animals made the transition to Australia intact.

The Chuckwagon

THE EARLY CATTLE DRIVES INTO British Columbia, from 1858 to 1868, were a time of learning for the drovers. The long journey from the river valleys of Oregon to the Cariboo goldfields were the first of the great cattle drives in North America. The great drives out of Texas did not take place until after the American Civil War. Although some of the drovers had been on the long overland trek along the Oregon Trail, herding a few head of cattle along with the long trains of Conestoga wagons was a relatively simple affair. But the drives into British Columbia, along narrow trails and with hundreds of head of cattle herded by a few men, were another story. The drovers had to learn from trial and error.

Supplies were usually packed on horses or mules, a wagon being impractical on the muddy, narrow trails. Food generally consisted of the bare essentials: flour, beans, and bacon. There was no awareness of scurvy, and drovers seldom packed fresh or dried vegetables or fruit. Some drovers would travel without the benefit of even a pack animal, carrying only a bedroll and a sack of beef jerky.

The cattle drives out of Texas from 1867 to 1887 saw many innovations in the techniques and tools for driving cattle. The open plains made it possible to load supplies and bedrolls on wagons and resulted in one of the greatest inventions in the cowboy world: the chuckwagon. Credit is given for the design of the chuckwagon to Charles Goodnight, one of the early Texas drovers who rebuilt a sturdy old army wagon and added the best idea of all, a chuck box. The chuck box perched at the back of the wagon and had a hinged lid that covered the part of the box that faced back and let down onto a swinging leg that formed a work table. When the lid was let down, a series of drawers were revealed that contained all of the essentials that a cook would need: utensils, pots, pans, condiments, and the all-important "possible drawer" that was a combination of first-aid kit and catch-all, holding everything from needle and thread to a bottle of whisky (for medicinal purposes for the cowboys, if not the cook).

While the rugged mountain terrain of British Columbia did not lend itself to chuckwagons, there were stretches of road where it was ideally suited. Cattle drives from the Cariboo and Chilcotin along the Cariboo Road used chuckwagons to carry all of the essentials for long drives to the markets of southern British Columbia and later to the railhead at Ashcroft. As well, the cowboys of the Douglas Lake Ranch would travel with a chuckwagon every spring to the Okanagan Valley to pick up cattle that had been purchased by the boss, J.B. Greaves. Starting in the South Okanagan or Similkameen, the drive would collect more and more cattle as it moved northward, eventually numbering up to a thousand head. The arrival of the Douglas Lake cowboys was always a special event among the isolated ranches of the Okanagan, and it was only with the coming of the railway to Vernon in 1892 that this picturesque sight became a thing of the past.

<<< **6** >>>

Cowboy Life

The Domesticated Cowboy

COWBOYS ARE GENERALLY HAPPIEST WHEN they are sitting in the saddle on a tall horse and working cattle. In fact, it might even be said that the cowboy, when off his horse, is not a cowboy at all. However, on the smaller ranches of the early days in particular, the cowboy was often called upon to perform a number of tasks that he might consider demeaning. Luckily, the cowboy was a loyal creature and, albeit begrudgingly at times, accepted the less romantic jobs like riding a hay mower instead of a horse or taking on the dreaded chore of fencing with barbed wire. While these jobs were at least performed outdoors, domestic duties were taboo to the average working cowboy. It was considered okay for a cowboy to cook up the grub for himself and his partner when sharing a cabin in a remote range for winter-feeding. In fact, some cowboys displayed a genuine talent for transforming the dried and powdered ingredients that were packed into the high country into quite passable fare. But when they were at the home site, the extent of their domestic duties was happily limited to washing up before dinner. Food preparation could be left to the cook, who was generally the wife of the rancher or an older retired cowboy who simply couldn't leave the ranching life.

But occasionally, even the most macho cowboy could not avoid kitchen duty, as Charlie Simms, who was working for Thomas Wood at his Winfield Ranch in the Okanagan, found out to his cost. It was the practice of the bachelor cowboys on Winfield Ranch to spend the weekend at Okanagan Mission, where the Lequimes ran an excellent stopping house and saloon. Each weekend, one cowboy had to stay behind to keep an eye on the cattle. So it fell that Charlie was asked to stay behind and, as Thomas Wood departed to town, was told to have some beans boiled and ready for Monday. Charlie, ever eager to please his boss, hunted around and found some beans and put them on to boil for a couple of hours. On Sunday morning, they did not seem to be cooked enough, so Charlie put them on to boil some more ... and some more. Sunday evening arrived, and the beans had not lost their flinty characteristics. When Tom Wood arrived home from town, he inquired whether Charlie had cooked the beans as requested. Charlie replied, "Well, Mr. Wood, I have been cooking some, but it seems to me they are taking an awfully long time to cook." Tom Wood had arrived in the Okanagan in 1867 and "batched" for many years, so he was reasonably experienced in the domestic arts. He remarked that sometimes beans were a little slow to get just right and perhaps a little soda would help. He lifted the lid and immediately uncovered the problem—Charlie had boiled up the winter supply of coffee beans. He was never asked to cook again.

Branding Time in the Nicola Valley

IN THE NICOLA VALLEY IN the 1930s, late May and early June was branding time. All the ranches that had cattle on the Hamilton Commonage would gather at the Douglas Lake Ranch's Hamilton corrals, southeast of the home ranch. Aside from the Douglas Lake Ranch, there would be representatives from the Guichon, Lauder, Abbott, and Sellers Ranches. Cowboys from each of the ranches worked together to round up over four thousand head of cattle spread across sixteen thousand acres of the commonage. Each ranch would show up with a crew of cowboys and a chuckwagon crammed with food, dishes, tents, bedrolls, branding irons, and much more. Sometimes a second wagon was needed to carry all the gear required for the job, which took weeks to accomplish. In addition, the ranches each brought a string of horses, and they were turned loose in an enclosed area to graze for the night.

Joe Coutlee, who had been cow boss at the Douglas Lake Ranch since the late 1890s, had overall charge of the round-up. In the early hours of the morning, well before dawn, Coutlee would holler—in a voice certainly designed to wake the dead—for the wranglers, who would mount the horses they had picketed for the night and head out in the dark to bring the horses into corrals. By then, a hearty breakfast of beefsteak, bacon, beans, bread, and coffee, would be ready. It would be served off the backs of the chuckwagons and the cowboys would eat in canvas tents by the light of coal oil lamps. Then they would head out and find their horse among the 150 or so in the corral, throw a loop over its head, saddle it, and mount, ready for the day's work.

Coutlee would divide the Hamilton Commonage into ten or twelve wedge-shaped sections and send riders to the far end of a new section each morning to sweep the area, gradually driving the cattle into the centre, where the mothers and calves would be matched up and pushed into corrals depending upon the mother's brand. Then, after a quick lunch, a thirty foot-long branding fire would be lit to accommodate all the different branding irons, and the work would begin. With several teams working at one time, the process was quick and efficient. When all the calves from one ranch were done, they were turned loose to join their mothers, who had been bellowing for their babies the whole time.

At the end of the branding, toward the end of June, the remaining cattle were driven to their respective ranches, and the Hamilton Commonage remained empty until the following spring. When all the cattle were established on their summer ranges in midsummer, Joe Coutlee would rise one morning and roar, "Today's Sunday!" Regardless of the day of the week, the cowboys, after seemingly endless seven-day weeks, would have some time off. Only a few cowboys would be needed to ride the summer range or to drive cattle to markets, so the rest of them would be laid off or added to the haying crews until it was time for fall round-up.

The Taboo against Milking

DESPITE BEING SURROUNDED BY THOUSANDS of head of cows, BC cowboys seldom had a supply of fresh milk. Cowboys would and could do almost everything with cattle: drive them, rope them, brand and castrate them, and many other jobs necessary to the cow business, but to ask them to milk cows? "No, sir." It was taboo to them. The average working cowboy would rather be caught dead than be found squatting down milking a cow.

Harry Marriott, who worked for the Gang Ranch, expressed surprise that, on unloading a freight wagon he had driven to the Gang Ranch, he saw a box of butter labelled "From New Zealand." "Afterwards I found out that, although the Gang Ranch had over seven thousand head of beef cattle, they did not go in for butter making... Cowboys and cattlemen have always shied away from cow milking, for some reason or another. It seemed to me that somewhere along the line it hurt their dignity somehow, as they regarded cow milking as one of the lowest down jobs that a human being could fall heir to doing." On the Gang Ranch, the Chinese cook would milk a few cows for his purposes, and any extra was fed to the pigs that the ranch kept for meat.

Hugh Walkem, who wrote a series of articles about BC ranches for the *Ottawa Citizen* in 1881, wrote about the lack of fresh milk: "The bachelors, who of course do not make butter, do not pretend to have milk either summer or winter, not because they cannot obtain milch [i.e. milk] cows, but I expect because it's too much trouble to milk, and as they become weaned, as it were, soon regard milk as a luxury rather than a necessary of life."

Some ranches, however, kept milk cows and, if there was no Chinese cook or "lady of the house" to do the milking, the cowboys would begrudgingly take a turn at milking after the day's work was done. Ed Carruthers, who worked as a ranch hand for the Lequime Ranch near present-day Kelowna, managed to avoid his turn because he was missing the middle two fingers on his right hand due to an accident as a boy. However, one Saturday evening, he was the only man not heading into Kelowna, so the foreman told him that he would just have to do the best he could. When he thought they had all left, he settled down to do the milking, which, of course, he was able to do quite well. He was disturbed from his task by the voice of the foreman yelling from behind him, "You so and so son of a gun [or words to that effect], so you can milk! Well, you'll do your share from now on." From then on, Carruthers had to accept his occasional stint at milking but, like all cowboys, he would rather have walked a mile on hot coals.

Killer Winters

CLIMATE PLAYED A CRUCIAL ROLE in the cowboys' daily life, whether they were feeding cattle through the long, dark months of winter or herding them in the blistering summer heat. And yet, despite the hardships that took their toll on young bodies, cowboys regarded the freedom of a life open to the elements as a privilege.

However, it is a hard fact of nature that winter is unpredictable. A winter that is devastating for one valley may be mild and open for the next valley over, or a late winter that sees no snow or cold by Christmas can turn nasty and last until May. Just when a rancher felt sure that his range was secure from winter's touch, a particularly hard winter might descend without warning and wipe him out. This was frequently the case in the interior of British Columbia.

In the early days, the ranchers put up hay using swamp grass or the native bunchgrasses and it was generally considered that a ton of hay per head was enough for winter feeding. Actual practice seems to indicate that much less hay than that was produced per head. In 1893, the North Okanagan had 5,200 head of cattle and 2,000 tons of hay produced. It is not surprising, then, that the occasional severe winter resulted in the starvation of great numbers of cattle. Typical was the severe winter of 1879–80, in which thousands of cattle died in the Thompson Okanagan. It is estimated that a full quarter of the 9000 cattle in the Nicola Valley perished before early April.

A severe winter that hit the Okanagan Valley in 1892–93 was described by Frank Buckland:

> Ranges and meadows were overstocked at normal times, so when a mild November and December dissolved into sub-zero [Fahrenheit] temperatures at the turn of the year, the winter-feed was soon exhausted. Week after week, the wind held in the north and by March, hay at any distant haul, was selling at $100 per ton, with all the haystacks in the valley cleaned up. By April hundreds of cattle were dead from starvation and cold. Others were so weak that they had to be helped to their feet in the morning before they could feed. Cowboys, one at the horns and one at the tail, had to jump for their horses the instant a critter was helped to its feet, because these wild range cattle would attack a man on foot even if it were their last lunge.

These severe winters, and others over the next twenty years, convinced ranchers of the need for large hay stocks to be put up for winter feeding. The cutting and stacking of hay during the summer months became part of the ranching scene that persists to the present day. While this practice increased ranchers' costs through the necessity for workers and equipment, it provided them with the insurance that cattle would have every chance to survive winters where snow and cold limited their chance for survival.

Barbed Wire—The Devil's Rope

FROM THE 1870S THROUGH THE 1890S, the cattle ranges of British Columbia stretched unfenced from the Cariboo-Chilcotin to the United States border. Cattle were turned loose in the spring and wandered wherever the grass led them. In the fall, the ranchers in a given area banded together to round up their cattle, brand the calves born in the summer, and move their cattle home for winter feeding.

But, as there were no fences to contain the cattle on their winter feeding grounds, they tended to drift with their backs to the wind, and winter storms could move cattle great distances. The *Vernon News* reported in January 1892 that a large number of cattle from Spallumcheen had drifted north to Grande Prairie (today's Westwold), where they were spotted and returned to their owners in the spring. The following year, which had one of the worst-ever winters in the North Okanagan, the cattle drifted in the opposite direction. It was reported in January that "A number of cattle bearing the brands of ranchers in the Spallumcheen were brought from the Mission [Kelowna] by Mr. John McCallum. Mac knows the brands of nearly all the breeders in the district and when cattle are gathered in for winter he sorts out the strays and restores them to their owners for a moderate fee." The incredible thing about this story is that the cattle had drifted unchecked for over seventy miles!

The coming of more and more settlers to British Columbia marked the end of the colourful open-range era. To keep the cattle out of farmers' fields or orchards, fences had to be constructed. Initially, heavy log fences such as the Russell or snake fence were built, but they proved costly. The obvious answer came from the new-fangled invention, "barbed wire," referred to by the ranchers and cowboys as "bobbed wire" or "the devil's rope."

As the latter term indicates, barbed wire was considered a plague by the cowboys. No job was more greatly despised than that of struggling to pull taut a wire loaded with sharp barbs ready to tear into the innocent cowboy's flesh. Barbed wire came in unwieldy rolls that added to the difficulty of the job. On one ranch in the Okanagan, the rolls were delivered on the beach from a scow and then had to be manhandled to the top of a steep bank before being loaded onto wagons. The rancher refused to use a horse to drag the rolls of barbed wire up the bank, insisting that it was easier and cheaper for the men to do the job. After wrestling a few rolls up the bank, one of the cowboys said in disgust, "To hell with this," and allowed a roll of wire to bounce down the hill and into the lake, narrowly missing the rancher on the way down. The roll of wire gathered considerable momentum in its downward trek and disappeared into the depths of the lake. After that, a horse was used for hauling the expensive wire up the bank.

The Galloping Game

A COWBOY'S LIFE WAS NOT all hard work and long hours. Quiet times on the ranch offered much-needed opportunities to let off steam and engage in the competitions and discussions typical of young men everywhere. Inevitably, the activities centred around horses and livestock and, not surprisingly, the competitions usually involved activities on horseback.

However, some of the games that the cowboys played were a little less predictable. For those who were of British extraction and spent most of their working days in the saddle, it seemed logical to organize games of polo. The first recorded game in Kamloops was played in 1890 and was an informal, fun match between eight local cowboys. There was no question about the cowboys' ability as horsemen, but striking the ball with the long-handled mallet proved to be more of a challenge—much to the amusement of the few spectators who came along for the fun. That first game ended with a 0-0 score, but practice makes perfect, and before long, the cowboys became more adept at the finer points of the game.

Polo was especially popular in the Nicola Valley at Nicola and Quilchena. Every Sunday afternoon, a match was organized at one of the two places, followed by a visit to the Quilchena Hotel or the Druid Hotel in Nicola. The countryside introduced a few natural hazards that may not be considered standard in what was affectionately called "the galloping game." One Sunday afternoon, the hot competition at Nicola came to an abrupt halt when a skunk made its leisurely way across the playing field. On another occasion, a coyote made the mistake of crossing the field, and the polo players immediately became "fox" hunters for the rest of the afternoon.

In 1896, the Nicola team was invited to Victoria to compete in what is considered the first polo tournament ever conducted in British Columbia. The team consisted of former British Army regulars Captain H.R. Cholmondelay, Captain A.C. Bald, and cowboys Broadbent and Nash, proving that true sportsmanship transcends class distinctions. The only difficulty was that the Nicola players, who had the wisdom and foresight to bring nine ponies along, had to ride and drive their horses fifty miles to the nearest railway station at Spences Bridge. They then had to travel by rail, sea, and road to arrive in Victoria three days later. Obviously, one of the team members must have had the money to support his enthusiasm and foot the bill for all the travel costs, but it all turned out very well when the Nicola team beat the Victoria and Cowichan teams and only narrowly lost by a single point to the Royal Navy team in the final few seconds of the game.

The Kamloops Polo Club was formed in 1897, with William Roper, who had a ranch at Cherry Creek as the honorary president. Roper enthusiastically supported the game and, in 1898, donated the Roper Cup, which he had brought in from England. Teams from all over the interior of British Columbia competed for the Roper Cup. Hugh Bayliff organized a team of Chilcotin cowboys that regularly competed, and teams from Grande Prairie (today's Westwold) also travelled to Kamloops to compete.

<<< **7** >>>

Chinese Participation in the Ranching Industry

Chinese Cowboy Kin Nauie

WHEN CONSTRUCTION OF THE CANADIAN Pacific Railway was completed in 1885, many of the Chinese who had worked on the construction settled in British Columbia and looked for meaningful employment. So it's not surprising that in the late 1800s and early 1900s, many of the ranches in British Columbia employed Chinese labourers during haying and harvesting and for irrigating. As well, Chinese workers were frequently hired as cooks on the round-up outfits. Eventually, these cooks proved to be capable and hard-working enough to be hired on by the large ranchers to cook for the home ranch. The records of the O'Keefe Ranch back into the 1890s show Chinese cooks in charge of preparing meals for the family and cowboys alike, and the Chinese cooks' bunkhouse still stands on the ranch.

The Chinese rarely worked on horseback, but a handful of Chinese ranch workers graduated to the job of cowboy and proved as indispensable at herding cattle as they were at cooking or agricultural tasks. One of these was Kin Nauie, who worked for years for the family of Alexander Graham, who had arrived in the Chilcotin in 1887. Graham's C1 Ranch at Alexis Creek was a going concern when Kin Nauie arrived in 1903. He found a job with Graham and spent the next thirty years working for the Graham family. Graham's daughter, Kathleen Telford, later described life in the remote Chilcotin in the early years of the 1900s: "While the men were away on these tedious cattle drives and freighting trips to Ashcroft, the women, children and hired hands kept the ranches going. The hired hands were usually Chinese and every large rancher employed one. They were loyal and efficient, working hard at jobs such as irrigating hayfields, milking cows, repairing ditches and flumes, and similar ranch chores. Our hired hand, Kin Nauie, remained with dad from 1903 to 1934 then returned to China."

During branding and fall cattle round-up and the occasional wild horse round-up, Kin Nauie would join the other cowboys on horseback and hold his own in the excitement and chaos of the chase. He also regularly assisted in moving cattle from summer to winter pasture and back in the spring. On one occasion, he was helping Graham push cattle across the Chilcotin River in sub-zero fall weather. Conditions were treacherous, and ice was forming on the rocks; Constable Robert Piper of the BC Provincial Police was helping the cowboys drive the cattle into the freezing Chilcotin when his horse slipped and went under. Graham threw Piper a rope, and he and his horse made it to shore, but Piper's prize Stetson went floating off down the river. No slouch with a rope, Kin Nauie neatly lassoed the hat and brought it safely to shore.

After thirty years with the Graham family, Kin Nauie returned to his family in China. But he missed the life on the ranches and returned to the Chilcotin two years later. Learning that his former boss, Alex Graham, had died, he hired on with Duke Martin at the old Graham Ranch and stayed for nearly twenty more years.

"Any Damned Thing"

EARLIER, WE LOOKED AT THE contribution that the Chinese made to ranching in the BC Interior. Although many of the Chinese who worked on ranches ended up as cooks for the cowboys who rode the range, a few graduated to become cowboys themselves.

Sin Tooie was another Chinese worker who successfully adapted to the cowboy life. Born in 1890, he was twenty years old when he left his home in Canton, China, and sailed to Canada to look for work. He took the train from Vancouver to Ashcroft and then headed for the Chilcotin. He was lucky enough to find a freight wagon headed for Hanceville that he could travel north with. As he later recounted, "I go with Indian freight wagon. We walked and walked and camped and camped. It rained. God damn it rained. We roll in blanket at night. No tent, no can get dry."

It took seventeen long days to reach Hanceville via the Gang Ranch. There he went to work for Alex Graham, no doubt at the urging of his countryman, Kin Nauie. He was a hard-working ranch hand, able to do anything asked of him, and later proudly recalled, "I cowboy, I work on irrigation ditches, I learn to cook, I mend machinery, I plough, I do any damn thing." He earned thirty dollars a month and worked ten hours a day. After saving his wages for two years, he returned to China, married, and then returned to Graham's.

By 1930, he was a cowboy at the Chilco Ranch and could rope and tie a calf with the best of them. But because of his versatility, he was still doing "any damn thing." He cooked for as many as twenty-seven men, mended mowing machinery, cut logs, butchered beef, and rode out looking for strays. During his stay in the Chilcotin, he returned to China five times and fathered two sons and two daughters. Neither his wife nor his children were allowed to come to Canada due to the discriminatory immigration laws in place at the time. He eventually owned his own café in Williams Lake.

Not all Chinese workers were relegated to the labour end of the ranching business. Some succeeded enough in other ventures to be able to purchase land and become ranchers. One example is Tong Sing, known to all by the name Joe Duck, who made enough money operating a store at Cache Creek to purchase a ranch in the Upper Hat Creek area. By the turn of the century, he was running close to two thousand head of cattle on his ranch and growing timothy and clover crops for feed. In 1907, the recently widowed Mrs. Kwan Yee took up a homestead to the south of the Duck Ranch. Kwan Yee moved in with Joe Duck a few years later, and her sons joined the working cowboys of the Duck Ranch. The Kwan boys looked after the cattle all winter, and their supply of excellent hay guaranteed that they would have fat cattle for sale all through the winter months. After the death of Kwan Yee in 1912, the sons continued to cowboy on the Duck Ranch but eventually left to further their education.

Gung Loy Jim and Little Fort Herefords

IN THE 1880S, RANCHERS BEGAN to look for ways of improving the Shorthorn–Spanish cross type of cows that had originally been driven into British Columbia from Oregon during the gold rush years. Some cattlemen decided to bring in a breed of cattle that was popular in Britain, the Hereford. So Hereford bulls were imported to breed with the mixed-breed cows. The resulting cattle were found to be able to withstand severe winters and produce excellent beef. More and more white-faced Herefords appeared, but the original Durham Shorthorns (mostly a roan colour) predominated, with a few Aberdeen Angus or Galloways in the mix.

As time went on, ranchers increasingly saw the Hereford as the best type of cattle for British Columbia conditions. By the mid-1930s and early 1940s, more and more ranchers were seeing that the use of purebred Hereford bulls was a way of ensuring consistency and rapid weight gain. Some ranchers saw the opportunity to raise purebred Hereford stock and, instead of selling their cattle for beef, to sell them for breeding. Gung Loy Jim was one of these purebred breeders.

Gung Loy Jim was the son of a storekeeper, Kam Kee, a second generation Chinese man who owned and operated the Jim Man Lee store in Mount Olie, later called Little Fort. In 1938, Loy started a fishing camp at

Taweel Lake but, because Chinese people were not allowed to lease crown land, he had to take a partner, Tom Humble, to take out the lease. The camp was so successful, attracting well-heeled people from all over the world, that he was able to fulfill his dream of raising purebred Herefords on land near Little Fort. Beginning in 1943 with six cows, he built up his herd of Little Fort Herefords. He continued improving the quality of his Herefords by the extensive use of artificial insemination and purchasing select cattle from the top herds in Canada. His bulls were his pride and joy and won several Grand Championships at the Kamloops Provincial Bull Sale. Loy was an astute judge of Hereford confirmation and, when ranchers were looking for large-framed, fast-growing cattle in the early 1970s to compete with the exotic breeds, he was recognized as one of the foremost breeders in the country, with cattle that had the genetic characteristics that ranchers were looking for. As he grew older, he spent his time working on the ranch and driving his tractor to oversee his beloved Herefords. Loy's eyesight began to fade, and his sons suggested that he stop driving the tractor because he couldn't see too well. He replied, "Hell, I know my way around the farm well enough to drive by the Braille method." His sons agreed that this was probably true, if you were not particularly concerned about gates and fences. In 1993, Gung Loy Jim was honoured at the Kamloops Bull Sale for his fifty years of membership in the Canadian Hereford Association. That year, he entered four bulls in the sale and took three first-place ribbons and one second, received Junior Champion, Junior Reserve Champion, Senior Champion, and Grand Reserve Champion honours. As well, his bulls won as Best Pair and the Best Group of Four class. His sons continue to raise Little Fort Herefords.

Chinese Cowboy Soldier

WEE TAN LOUIE WAS A native-born British Columbian of Chinese parentage whose father, Chee Ah Louie, had arrived in California in 1849 for the gold rush and ended up in British Columbia. After a stint working on the construction of the Canadian Pacific Railway, he started working at the Sullivan Ranch near the present town of Chase. Wee Tan grew up there and spent much of his early life working on the nearby ranches. In 1914, he was working as a cowboy for the Douglas Lake Ranch when he heard that Canada was at war with Germany. Wee Tan, who spoke and wrote excellent English, was a rugged individual and accomplished horseman. So he was determined to enlist in the Canadian Expeditionary Force and fight for his country. But things were getting worse for the Chinese in those days. As soon as the CPR was completed, the federal government had moved to restrict the immigration of Chinese people to Canada. The first federal anti-Chinese bill was passed in 1885. It took the form of a head tax of $50 imposed, with few exceptions, upon every person of Chinese origin entering the country. The head tax was increased to $100 in 1900 and to $500 in 1903. Five hundred dollars was equivalent to two years wages of a Chinese labourer at the time. Meanwhile, the Chinese were denied Canadian citizenship.

Nonetheless, Wee Tan rode to Kamloops and went to the enlistment office. But he was refused. "Orientals" were not allowed to enlist, as they were not considered citizens. Wee Tan tried several times but was turned down every time. However, it seemed that British Columbia was the worst province for the Chinese in Canada, and other provinces were more open to Chinese enlistment. So, in the fall of 1917, he had saved enough to purchase a horse and supplies and set out to Calgary to try his luck there. The journey took three months and, as winter closed in, the going was particularly rough through freezing temperatures and blizzards. But he persevered and reached Calgary in February. Wanting to make sure this time, Wee Tan gave his name as William Thomas, a name he had spotted on a mailbox and, on February 20, 1918, was accepted into the 10th Canadian Infantry Battalion. He arrived in Bamshot, England, in April and, after basic training, crossed the channel into the war zone. Because he was so quick on his feet, he served as a runner and, over the next seven months, served in France, Holland, and Belgium. Wee Tan returned to Canada in March 1919 and was honourably discharged after receiving the British War Medal and the Victoria Medal. Ironically, upon his return to British Columbia, his status had not changed. He was not allowed to purchase land or to vote in elections. It would not be until 1947 that Wee Tan was even allowed to vote in the country for which he had fought and risked his life.

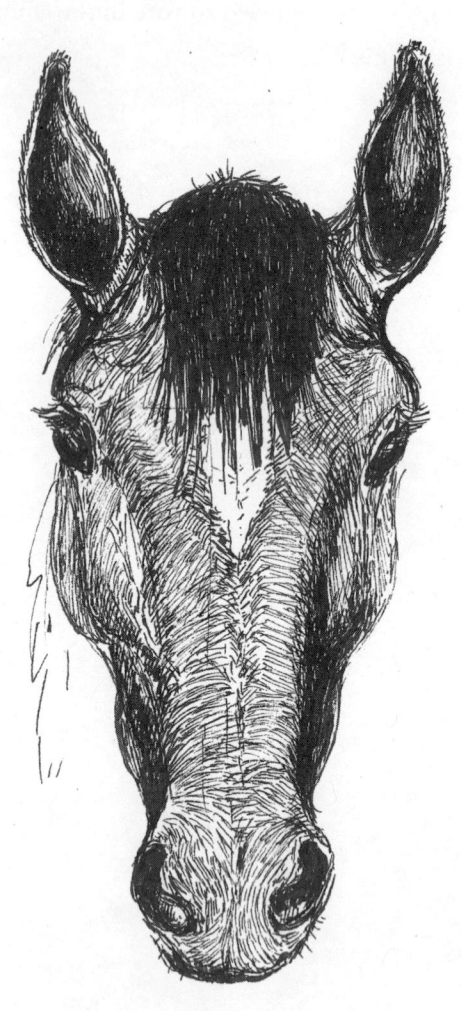

<<< **8** >>>

Horses

Cayuses

AN OLD-TIME COWHAND ONCE SAID, "Cowboys is noisy fellers with bow legs and brass stomachs that rides hosses and hates any kind of work they can't do on one." The cowboy and the horse have been inseparable since the beginning of the cattle trade in North America. British Columbia, where the open ranges stretched unfenced from the United States border to the Cariboo-Chilcotin in the early days, was no different. Cattle roamed free and spent much of their time in a half-wild state. The only way to handle these wild range cattle was on horseback, for a man on foot was at the mercy of their sharp horns and pounding feet.

The working cow horses of the early years were small, seldom over fourteen hands high and no more than six hundred pounds in weight, but powerful. They could run all day and then kick off the hat of their rider at night. They were descended from the Barb horse of North Africa that the Moors had brought to fight in Spain in 711 A.D. Unlike the bulky, powerful horses of northern Europe, these horses, bred in the hot dry countryside of North Africa and Andalusia, were lean, sinewy, and energetic. The Spanish then brought horses to Mexico in the 1500s, and here they found an environment similar to that of their native North Africa.

These horses then moved northward through Texas onto the plains and through California into the mountains and wet climate of the northwest. In Oregon and the Great Basin area, the horses changed subtly, becoming stockier and heavier, perhaps due to the influence of the French Breton horses brought to the area by the French-Canadian fur traders. On the ranges of the northwest, the wild horses generally became known as "cayuses," a term unknown in the south or east of the Rockies. It derived from the Cayuse people in eastern Washington and Oregon, who were noted for their expert horsemanship and careful breeding of these small, strong horses. The term came north with the early drovers and miners and came to refer to any wild horse that could be broken for ranch work. Over time, their use spread east of the Rocky Mountains, but in the early days, it appears to have been unique to the northwest.

In the interior of British Columbia, cayuses found another environment that particularly suited their constitution. Extensive grasslands and hot, dry summers resembled the southern climates from whence they had come, and the cold winters were still mild enough that horses could survive by pawing away the snow in the sheltered valleys. Soon cayuses were at home in British Columbia and joined those that had escaped from the Indigenous people and the fur traders in earlier years to form large herds of wild horses. The ranchers and cowboys of the Interior saw these herds as the ready material that they needed to carry on their business. The thrill of the wild-horse chase and the toughness and skill of the horse breaker became a part of the cowboy way of life in British Columbia.

Hugh B. Walkem, son of the premier of British Columbia, wrote an article for the *Ottawa Citizen* in 1881, later copied in the *Inland Sentinel* (then published in Yale) in which he described the "cayoosh," which was his term for the cayuse:

> The general purpose horse of this region, however, is a "cayoosh," a small, but hardy native animal. Now the term "cayoosh" is a term of

reproach, for instance if you want to make a particularly disagreeable remark concerning your neighbour's horse, just call it a "mean cayoosh," a term which implies all the vices and defects that horse-flesh is heir to. But after all the much-despised "cayoosh" is a very useful animal, and it is the mode of breaking and abusing him that makes him mean and vicious, as he generally has much less pains taken with his education than his more dignified brother, the imported American horse. The "cayoosh" is superior to the latter as a stock horse, for he is more active and not being so valuable you do not loose very much if you in any way injure him, and it does not take very long to "stiffen him up" to use a trite expression, for driving stock necessitates a great deal of hard riding.

In the days of the open range, ranchers began to import more notable breeds of horses in an effort to combine the stamina of the cayuse with the size of the larger breeds. John Gilmore of the Nicola Valley brought in two half-Norman dapple grey mares, three and four years old, to use for breeding stock to upgrade the working horses of the Nicola. Gilmore's lead was followed by some other ranchers in the Nicola Valley, including Lawrence Guichon, John Hamilton, the Moore brothers, and the Mickle brothers. The overall effect was to add size to the stamina that had characterized the cayuses of the past.

As the quality of horses grew in the BC Interior, events were unfolding elsewhere that would make these hardy range horses much in demand. During the early 1880s, as railway construction advanced across the prairies, cattle ranching was starting up in a big way in the southern grasslands of the North-West Territories, the future Alberta and Saskatchewan. Demand for horses in these areas was great, and the ranches of Montana could not supply anywhere nearly enough horses. At the same time, the ranchers of southern British Columbia knew that there was an abundance of horses in the hills and upland areas of the province and acted quickly to profit from their knowledge. Between 1883 and 1885, thousands of horses were driven east from the grasslands of BC.

Horses of the Pacific Northwest

ON HIS SECOND TRIP TO North America in 1494, Christopher Columbus dropped anchor off the north coast of Hispaniola, Haiti, and unloaded twenty-four stallions and ten mares. They were the first of their kind in the western hemisphere, and their descendants would dramatically change life in the New World. These horses were descended from the Barb horses of North Africa that the Moors brought with them when they fought Spain in 711 AD. They were unlike the heavy, powerful horses of Northern Europe that had been bred to pull a plough or carry a knight in armour. They were raised primarily for riding in the hot, dry climate of North Africa and Spain and were lean and quick, qualities that were especially favourable both for combat and for chasing the half-wild cattle of Andalusia.

The conquistadors brought horses in 1519 to the mainland of Mexico, where the short grasses and unbounded plains and mountains made them even wirier. Over the next centuries, these small, wiry horses escaped from their owners and wandered northward into territory that would become the United States. In their wild state, they grew as fleet as deer and as strong as oxen. Generation after generation of horses lost size and gained "wind." What they lost in beauty, they gained in utility. They were made for running and making quick turns, and their lungs, expanded from generations of freedom, gave them the ability to run all day.

These superbly conditioned horses moved northward onto the Great Plains and through California into the mountainous and wet climate of the northwest. In Oregon and the Great Basin area, they encountered larger horses that had descended from the Norman and Breton breeds introduced into New France and used by the fur traders who moved into the area in the early 1800s. The result was a stockier, heavier horse that still possessed the speed and stamina of the Spanish breeds. The Hudson's Bay Company (HBC) in Oregon Country (today's Oregon, Washington, and British Columbia) used these horses to carry trade goods into and furs out of northern British Columbia. By the 1840s, the HBC had established breeding programs at some of its forts in the Pacific Northwest, including Fort Kamloops. As the Company needed large horses that could carry heavy packs, not riders, the horses were bred for size, something that the French Norman and Breton horses were known for. This gave them strength and endurance. As the fur trade employees, mostly French Canadians, left the HBC and took up land in the Pacific Northwest, they brought these horses with them. Their bloodlines were further enhanced by the introduction of new breeds, notably Morgans and thoroughbreds, brought by settlers from the eastern US over the Oregon Trail. Before long, the horses of the Pacific Northwest were acknowledged as among the finest on the continent.

With the signing of the Oregon Treaty in 1846 between Britain and the US, the territory south of the forty-ninth parallel was lost to the HBC. The Company's forts south of the border were instructed to move their cattle and horses north to Fort Kamloops, where the bunchgrass ranges were plentiful. As a result, the HBC moved a large number of horses, including two hundred brood mares, to Kamloops, where they flourished. A large number of the horses escaped into the wild and added a genetic boost to the wild horses already in the area. In the years to come, a ready market for these horses was found on the Canadian Prairies.

Wild Horses in the Okanagan

DURING THE EARLY YEARS OF the twentieth century, British Columbia experienced a tremendous population growth, and newcomers to the province moved into all the areas that could possibly be used for farming. The increasing number of farms and ranches sparked a demand for horses, and prices reflected the growing value for good stock. For many of the young cowboys, the wild horses found in the remote areas of the Interior looked like easy money to be made during slack time at the ranches. The horses were considered fair game and, as long as they did not carry anyone's brand, they were "slick ears," a name more properly referring to calves with no earmark or brand. However, it was not a task for an amateur. Catching wild horses in the rough backcountry required a sure-footed saddle horse, knowledge of the terrain, and a combination of determination and luck.

The South Okanagan was home to large bands of wild horses. As early as 1833, David Douglas had referred to the "River of Wild Horses" in the South Okanagan. He probably meant the Marron River, as the term "marron" comes from the French meaning "feral or wild." Wild horses roamed the area from Marron Lake past Aeneas Lake on both sides of the valley. The country provided excellent bunchgrass range as well as watering holes and salt licks for them. Many of them were fine horses, descended from stock that had escaped from immigrants or local ranches.

Farther south, at Kruger Mountain, there were hundreds of wild horses in the years before the First World War. At Tule Lake on Kruger Mountain, there was a huge corral, built from good-sized logs, with wings extending half a mile in each direction to funnel the horses into the corral. Springtime, just after the snow had melted, was the accepted time for wild horse roundups, before the tough little animals recovered their strength after pawing through snow for their feed all winter. Mounted on sure-footed cow ponies that had been well fed all winter, the cowboys tried to run the wild horses into the large log corral.

Wild horses also abounded east of the Okanagan Valley along the Dewdney Trail in the Kettle Valley. The McMynn family ranched in the Midway area and frequently hunted wild horses. One particular band was led by an escaped stallion that, unlike the small, stocky wild horses, stood sixteen hands high and weighed about twelve hundred pounds. Every attempt to corral this magnificent stallion had failed. Each summer, Billy and Jim McMynn organized a horse hunt and, on one occasion, managed to corral the stallion, whose vision was so obscured by dust that he did not see the corral. He was trapped along with about two hundred head of wild horses. The McMynns offered twenty head of horses to anyone who could break the stallion, so Arthur Kean and his brother, Albert, thought they would give it a try. They drove him into a small corral. There, they roped his forefeet and tumbled him to tie him down and then saddle him. Arthur Kean mounted him and went for the ride of his life. The stallion bucked and reared and turned his head to try and bite Kean's feet, but he stayed on, with his brother herding the horse to keep him from hitting the corral fence. That first ride lasted about an hour and a half before the exhausted horse and rider called it quits. Several months later, the stallion was fully broken and turned out to be a superb saddle horse.

Wild Horses in the Chilcotin

BY THE EARLY 1900s, countless wild horses inhabited the Chilcotin, especially on the ranges north of the Chilcotin River. Alexander Gillespie, who worked as a rider for the Gang Ranch, recalled a wild horse round-up in the spring of 1903, when a Mr. Hawden of Duncan purchased 250 head from the Gang Ranch, to be rounded up and delivered to Ashcroft. Hawden confidently expected to find a market for the scrubby wild horses in Toronto, so the Gang Ranch agreed to come up with them.

All the Chilcotin people in the neighbourhood participated in the hunt with the local ranchers, all expecting to make a few dollars for their efforts. The drive began at daylight because the horses were in the open then, usually seeking the protection of the timber during daylight hours to avoid flies and predators. A large group of cowboys under the leadership of an experienced hand would surround one of the small open valleys, common in that country, where there would be one or two bands of horses feeding. The surrounding had to be done with the utmost caution, as the mere breaking of a branch would send the spooked horses into the timber, where it would be impossible to move them. Cowboys were placed at the head of the trails into the timber to turn back the horses into the open valley bottom when the main group of men appeared at one end of the valley. Then the chase would begin, with everyone riding at a full gallop as the wild horses were headed out into an open area where they could be surrounded and held until they settled down enough to be manageable. The whole herd would be driven off towards a huge figure-eight-shaped log corral where they could be sorted out, with the branded horses either being taken away by their owners or turned out to range again. The wild, unbranded "slick ears" were run into the adjoining corral and held there.

The hunt for wild horses lasted for nearly a month and, when the required number of horses was obtained, they had to be driven to Ashcroft. The cowboys assigned to the drive had their hands full, especially on the first day, which involved crossing the Chilcotin River. At first, the horses refused to enter the water and began to mill, threatening to stampede. Eventually, the lead mares were headed into the river and the rest followed. After a few days, the horses settled into the routine and were relatively easy to handle, as they kept together and did not try to break away.

The drive proceeded down the Cariboo Road for ten days, encountering freight wagons and pack trains along the way. The horses churned up thick dust and covered horses and riders alike with a uniform coating. At Ashcroft the horses were put into stock corrals and then run up a chute into the cattle cars. Fifteen carloads of horses left Ashcroft and headed east under the careful eye of Mr. Hawden and a few cowboys who stayed to handle the horses at the end of the railway trip. As it turned out, Hawden decided to sell them in Calgary and received a good price for them from Alberta ranchers hungry for good mounts. The cowboys who had stayed with him from the beginning received the sum of ninety dollars for their efforts.

"BC Horses"

IN THE EARLY 1880s, the ranchers of British Columbia were closely watching the developments across the mountains. When the Canadian government opened vast areas of land for ranching leases in 1881, it was obvious that a ranching industry would develop that would soon eclipse the one in British Columbia. But the good news was that the ranchers there would need good-quality cattle and horses. In both of these categories, British Columbia was second to none. And, even though there was lots of livestock available in Montana, the quality of that stock was generally inferior to British Columbia's, especially the horses. On the open range, each cowboy had eight or more horses for round-up: tough circle horses for rounding up, a sure-footed gentle pony for night riding, a cutting horse for working herds, a roping horse, and a good horse for swimming rivers. Most of all, cowboys were looking for horses that could handle large, heavy cattle and preferred the bigger BC stock over the smaller American cow ponies. Drovers like Adam Ferguson and Jim Christie, who had driven horses through the Yellowhead Pass in 1874, and John Shaw, who had driven the first commercial cattle onto the prairies through the North Kootenay Pass in 1875, had proven that the Rocky Mountains were not a barrier. By the 1880s, better trails were being developed through the mountains, particularly the Crowsnest Pass, which opened the primary ranching area to the east. During the 1880s, there was a huge influx of British Columbia horses and horsemen to Alberta.

In 1882, Oscar Rush, who worked for Johnny Wilson of the JW Ranch in Grande Prairie (now Westwold), drove 150 horses through the Okanagan Valley. The herd was then crossed into the United States at Osoyoos and given a temporary permit to cross US territory on the way east. Normally a special envoy accompanied the herd through the US at a cost to the drovers of four dollars a day plus expenses to ensure that the horses were not sold in the US without customs duty being charged. Rush and his cowboys drove the herd down the Okanogon River (as it was spelled in the US) to Omak Lake and then across the Colville Indian Reservation. The herd was swum across the Columbia River and then via Spokane Falls to cross back into Canada at Bonners Ferry. From there they travelled through the Crowsnest Pass to Fort Macleod, where they were broken. When Rush heard that the Oxley Ranch was looking for horses, he drove them to the Garnett brothers' ranch, near Pincher Creek, where he held them for inspection. John Craig, manager of the Oxley Ranch, was impressed and bought 116 of them. Craig later noted, "The first purchase of stock for the Oxley Ranch was a band of 116 horses from a Mr. Rush, who had brought them in from British Columbia and was holding them at Garnett's ranch. They were a very good sort, and cost seventy dollars per head."

The ranchers in the area were impressed with the quality of the horses. One wrote, "These 'BC horses,' as they were locally called, were derived from Morgan and thoroughbred crosses on Spanish foundation stock. Exceptionally active, good looking mounts, they were big and tough as rawhide." This reputation was to make "BC horses" particularly valued in the next few years and would allow the ranchers of British Columbia to sell off a large portion of their excess horses in southern Alberta.

When word got back to the British Columbia Interior that there was a good market for horses in the North-West Territories (as the Canadian prairies were called until 1905), others were prompted to get involved. In the spring of 1883, William Roper Hull, who had come to British Columbia from Somersetshire, England, in 1873 with his brother John, decided to try driving horses to the North-West. The brothers purchased twelve hundred head of horses, a number of them from the BX Ranch in the Okanagan Valley. They drove them south along Okanagan Lake and through Washington Territory, then back across the Tobacco Plains and through the Crowsnest Pass to the prairies. When they arrived at Fort Macleod, the herd was greeted with enthusiasm. Out of the herd, three hundred horses were sold to Fred Stimson of the North West Cattle Company, which ran the Bar U Ranch southwest of Calgary.

While the horse drives seemed like a way to earn easy money, they weren't always simple. As straightforward as it may sound, driving horses is far from easy. Usually, a large band of horses included mares in foal or with colts, making travel slow. If mares foaled on the trail, they usually wanted to stay where they were and had to be urged along. Occasionally, the entire herd would grow homesick and head for home, making night-herding essential. Cowboys had to ride around the herd at night and turn back horses if they headed back down the trail. The horses' tendency to want to return to their home territory was accentuated when the herd was forced to swim across a river, or on a rainy night, making the cowboy's life miserable. Most old-timers agreed that a herd of horses was much more likely than a herd of cattle to stampede. The merest whiff of a cougar or whisper of an unfamiliar sound could send the herd into a mad panic, and woe betide the cowboy who got in their way.

The influx of BC horses continued and, even after the railway was completed in 1885, there was a demand for British Columbia horses and cattle in the North-West Territories. William and John Roper Hull, after driving horses into the North-West Territories for several years, decided that they would set up a butchering and livestock-trading business in Calgary. That spring, the first consignment of stock ever shipped into the North-West Territories by rail from British Columbia arrived in Calgary. By the end of the year, they had brought in from British Columbia five hundred horses and three thousand head of cattle.

That same year, Senator Matthew Cochrane travelled to Ashcroft, BC, and met with Thaddeus Harper, who was looking to liquidate his assets to cover a growing debt load. Cochrane was interested in Harper's horses, located on the Gang Ranch, with the intention of selling them to the British cavalry. He ended up purchasing five hundred of them and had them shipped by rail to his newly incorporated British American Ranch Company. The Gang Ranch horse herd, referred to as the Harper Band, was considered "one of the finest in the West." Unfortunately, the British cavalry did not purchase the horses, but the Bow River Horse Ranch, with the Harper Band as part of its foundation stock, operated successfully until after the First World War.

Interest in BC horses continued for some time. But, in 1890, the Canadian Pacific Railway shipped sixty-six horses from Alberta to the British Columbia market, indicating that the tide was beginning to turn. However, for the better part of ten years, the ranges of the British Columbia Interior had provided horses and horsemen to the fledgling cattle industry in the North-West Territories. In the process, many of the horse-breaking techniques and much of the horse equipment of the west coast had been imported as well.

"Wild Horse" Johnson

ONE OF THE COWBOYS WHO drove the JW horses with Oscar Rush through the Crowsnest Pass in 1882 was a young man in his early twenties named Edward Johnson. He had been born in Hampshire, England, and left home at the age of fourteen to work for the largest horse-breaking and sales stable in the south of England. After a couple of years there, he worked as a deckhand on the full-rigged sailing ship *Selvedere* and arrived in Valparaíso, Chile, where he secured a job breaking horses for the Chilean army. After that, he took a boat north to Victoria, British Columbia, and travelled to the Interior. He soon got a job breaking horses for a ranch in the Ashcroft area before getting a job with the JW Ranch in Grande Prairie in 1881. Johnson's extensive experience in breaking wild horses inspired someone to give him the nickname Wild Horse.

After driving the JW horses to Alberta, Johnson decided to move to Alberta in 1887. At that time, there was still a demand for quality horses, and Wild Horse and his friend Charles Berry contracted with J. Dean of the Herd Ranch on the Elbow River to go back to BC and capture five hundred wild horses and ship them to Calgary. By then, the Canadian Pacific Railway had been completed and made livestock shipping a simple matter compared with the pre-railway days. But catching wild horses was not a job for the faint of heart.

Johnson and Berry travelled to the Big Bar Creek area along the Fraser River, where there was an abundance of wild horses on the open ranges. The two men arrived on the range in the early spring, when the wild horses were at their weakest, having scratched through the snow all winter for feed. In the spring, while there was still snow on the ground, a big, healthy, grain-fed horse could outrun the wild horses. Johnson and Berry built a stout corral. Then they located a band of wild horses and drove them for miles until they could be funnelled into the corral. It took nerve and a fine horse to drive a bunch of wild horses through the brush and timber, and bruises and scrapes were guaranteed. Once the horses were in the corral, came the job of breaking the horses.

Slowly but surely, the wild horses were "green broke" so that they could be trained into tough, hardy saddle horses, but their wild horse instincts remained. They were carefully herded into Ashcroft, where they were loaded into stock cars bound for Calgary. Johnson and Berry returned with the horses and delivered them to the Herd Ranch. The two men then headed back to Calgary to spend some of their hard-earned money, and there Johnson met Mandella Midthrone, whom he married in the fall of 1888. That winter, the newlyweds travelled to British Columbia, where Wild Horse drove a BC Express stagecoach on the Cariboo road.

The Johnsons returned to Alberta in the spring of 1888, and Wild Horse worked for the Oxley Ranch through the summer and during fall round-up. In 1903, he moved to Midnapore, where he built the Dominion Hotel, which he ran for a few years. But his first love was horses, so, in 1913, Johnson leased a small place west of Okotoks where he could raise his family and indulge in his favourite activity, raising and breaking horses. He and his two sons, Sam and Bill, who were also cowboys, helped to organize the first rodeo in Black Diamond in 1915. Wild Horse later moved back to Midnapore, where he finished off his days. He died in 1949 at the age of ninety-one, one of the last original old-time horse breakers.

Dependence and Respect

THE STORY OF THE COWBOY is interwoven with two types of animals: cattle, the source of their income, and horses, their working partners. Both of these animals arrived in Hispaniola in 1493 with the Spanish explorers and soon made their way through Central America and Mexico. Since that time, ranching has depended upon the horse and cow for its livelihood. The gradual improvement of the breeds of cattle and horses has been an important part of the continued survival of the ranching industry in North America.

Since they depended so much upon both horses and cattle, it is not surprising that the early cowboys treated them with great care. Cattle were their "bread and butter" and any cowboy who handled them roughly or ran them needlessly, was sent "down the road" in short order. The same applied to horses. All of the horses belonged to the ranch, and any cowboy who abused his horse was not around for long. Today's working cowboy is no different. At the Ranch Rodeo that takes place every year at the O'Keefe Ranch Cowboy Festival, the true skill of the cowboy or cowgirl and their horse is demonstrated. To watch the gentle way in which cattle are handled and the incredible working team that the cowboy and horse make is to see a true bond of mutual dependence and respect.

This is not to say that the cowboy does not need to spur his horse at times or bump and rope the cattle to make them cooperate. To an outsider, this may appear rough but, make no mistake, the care of his animals is paramount to the cowboy. But, on occasion, someone less familiar with the way of the cowboy might be concerned.

This is illustrated in the story of when J.B. Greaves, Manager of the Douglas Lake Ranch, was at the Thomas Wood Ranch, at the foot of Wood Lake, gathering cattle to drive north. Mrs. Wood was watching at the corral one day when she saw one of the Indigenous cowboys, nicknamed Buckskin Joe, spurring his horse's flanks while trying to head off an uncooperative cow. Mrs. Wood, an active member of the Society for the Prevention of Cruelty to Animals, was not impressed and threatened to have the man arrested for cruelty to his horse. Greaves was keen to avoid trouble and agreed to send the man over in the morning so Mrs. Wood could give him a good talking-to. However, to avoid any fireworks, Greaves convinced Joe Coutlee to pose as Buckskin. Coutlee, the son of a French father and Indigenous mother, was a man with a sense of humour and the courteous charm associated with the French. Coutlee rode to the house and stood politely as Mrs. Wood went up one side of him and down the other. Finally, he promised graciously that it would never happen again and departed, much to the delight of his fellow cowboys.

Horse Culture

FROM THE FIRST DAYS OF ranching in the North-West Territories, as the Canadian Prairies were known in the late 1800s, ranchers and cowboys alike recognized and acknowledged the superiority of the horses bred west of the Rockies. Fred Ings, who had worked as a cowboy on the 1883 round-up and later owned the Midway Ranch, wrote in his memoirs, "We needed good horses and big ones; we never rode small horses like the American cowboy. Our cattle were larger and we needed the size and weight." This need for larger horses to handle the large purebred cattle that were being brought into the North-West Territories was recorded in the 1913 book, *The Range Men*:

> The range stock of the South-West, of Texas, New Mexico, and Old Mexico, is quick, light, and as speedy as most horses, while the range animals of Alberta and Montana are grade Shorthorns and Herefords, huge, clumsy, well-fed brutes, whose best gait is a lumbering gallop, and whose agility compared with that of the Mexican steer is as a tortoise to a hare. Canadian stock was half as big again as the South-Western range beasts, twice as slow, and not a quarter as agile. A Canadian rope-horse was picked for strength and weight to oppose the

weight and strength of the heavy steers; the Arizona and Texas and other American steeds were picked for speed, sure-footedness, and dodging ability.

The "BC horses" brought in from across the Rockies fit the bill for strength and weight and were universally accepted as the best horses on the southern prairies. Not surprisingly, along with the horses came horse-breaking techniques. The use of the hackamore, derived from the Spanish *jaquima*, was widespread in British Columbia and spread to the North-West Territories. The method of breaking horses with a hackamore can be traced back to the *vaqueros* of California. The use of a hackamore was considered by most California "buckaroos" (as the term *vaquero* was pronounced by the English-speaking cattlemen) to produce a soft-mouthed horse, responsive to the reins. Once a horse was trained with a hackamore, it was usually replaced with a bit. This technique was unheard of on the Great Plains, where a bit was the standard piece of equipment in horse breaking. So it would seem that the California methods of horse breaking travelled to the North-West Territories via Oregon, Washington State, and British Columbia.

In the area of horses and horse equipment, the influence on the cattle culture of Alberta from British Columbia was pronounced. The large, tough horses of these regions were just what were needed for the improved breeds of cattle that were larger and slower than the Texas longhorns that had come as far as Montana, with few of them making it into the North-West Territories. Along with the horses came certain aspects of the buckaroo horse culture. Certainly, the methods of breaking horses seem to have been readily accepted in the Territories, and the use of the hackamore was very popular. Other aspects of the horse culture, namely single-cinched saddles and braided rawhide ropes, were less prominent.

"7U" Brown

JOSEPH HARRISON BROWN WAS BORN in Ashfield, County Cavan, Ireland, in 1856 and, at an early age, emigrated to Canada with his family, settling in Peterborough, Ontario.

Brown left Ontario in 1882, sailing around the Horn and arriving in British Columbia that same year. He travelled to the BC Interior, where he managed to land a job at a lumber mill. He did not prove adept at the job and one day, while piling lumber in a shed, he dropped a plank on the foreman's head. The irate foreman headed up one side of the scaffolding and Brown headed down the other, never looking back. And so Joseph Brown ended his career in the lumber industry.

Eventually, he got a job at the BX Ranch in the North Okanagan, where the stagecoach horses were raised. Brown proved to be very talented in handling the highly charged BX horses and in training them. But, once again, his career took a turn. In 1883, he was assigned the task of seeing twelve hundred BX horses across the mountains to the North-West Territories. Three hundred of these horses were purchased by the North West Cattle Company for the Bar U Ranch, and Brown was in charge of delivering them. His adeptness with the horses impressed Fred Stimson, the Bar U manager, who hired him on the spot to break and care for the horses. For the next fifteen years, he was in charge of the Bar U's horses.

By 1886, Brown had saved enough to buy a small herd of fifty heifers and go into partnership with Bar U neighbour Frank Bedingfeld, who had arrived with his mother, Agnes, in 1884. The partners picked the brand 7U for their cattle. Given the number of Browns on the southern North-West ranges, Joseph soon became known as 7U Brown, a name that was so universally used that most people forgot—or never knew—his first name. Brown then chose to use the BX brand for his horses in memory of his first employer in the ranching business.

Brown's attitude toward ranching was definitely old school. He believed that his cattle, apart from his calves, should be able to rustle for enough to keep themselves alive through the winter. He swore that, if he could get through the winter on whisky, his stock could survive on snow. And there is no question that whisky was one of his main food groups. He always had jugs or even cases hidden in various places on the ranch, in haystacks, or in outbuildings. Despite his prodigious consumption, he never missed a day's work in his life and considered the cost of whisky to be a necessary operating expense.

Brown was still actively ranching at the age of seventy-one when he had a serious accident. His horse fell, breaking Brown's leg and tearing his scalp open. Undeterred, Brown had a cowboy cut a willow post and tie it in place above and below the break and then pulled his hat down on the side of his head to hold the scalp in place. The frontier doctoring complete, he rode back to the ranch for more extensive repairs. Brown died in 1936 at the age of 80.

"My Horse Is Faster Than Yours!"

GIVE A MAN A HORSE and he will ride it. Give two men each a horse and they will want to know which one is fastest. Horse racing began in British Columbia almost as soon as the first horses arrived, and any gathering of people from then on usually involved a horse race.

Tom Stevenson, who cowboyed for the Postill Ranch at the south end of Duck Lake in the 1880s, tells the story of a famous race that took place near Priest's Valley (now Vernon) on Victoria Day, May 24, 1887. The race was between Alf Postill's "Roney" and Louis Bercier's "Mountain Chief," and all the old-time ranchers turned up chatting and exchanging news. Excitement ran high and the betting even higher as race time approached. Stevenson, who had helped to train Roney, found that, before he knew it, he had bet most of his winter wages on his favourite. As he headed away from the noisy bunch of bettors, he met an Okanagan cowboy with a little Appaloosa stock horse that he was willing to bet on Mountain Chief. Stevenson tried to wager his own saddle horse for the Appaloosa, but instead the Indigenous man eyed his new double-rigged Cheyenne saddle and offered to bet his horse for the saddle. Off came the saddle, straight onto the Appaloosa, winner take all.

Cornelius O'Keefe, who owned most of the land on either side of the race area, paced off a mile-long stretch along the Okanagan Landing road. E.J. Tronson, Okanagan Chief Paul, and Price Ellison acted as judges. Finally, the horses were off. At the quarter, Mountain Chief led by four lengths with Bercier laying on the quirt. Postill rode low and easy, not laying a hand on Roney. At the half, Bercier looked to be pulling away as he was six lengths ahead, still laying on the whip. By the three-quarter mark, his lead was reduced to three lengths, but Postill was riding hard and gaining. In the stretch, with Bercier still a length in front, spectators began to close in from behind, shooting their six-guns in the air. Now both riders were laying on the quirt as they crossed the finish line, with Roney in the lead by half a length. Stevenson was all smiles as he swung up on his new Appaloosa horse and rode off.

More races followed as the afternoon passed and, in the evening, the furniture was moved out of the dining room in Tronson's Victoria Hotel to allow for dancing until daybreak. The few Indigenous and white women present were in high demand, as each cowboy was determined to dance as often as possible. As the grey dawn was breaking, a tired but happy throng of cowboys mounted up and headed off to their respective ranches for a hard day's work. Happiest of all was Stevenson as he rode tall in the saddle of his new stock horse.

Horses for the War Effort

HORSES WERE WIDELY USED IN the first years of the First World War, both for mounted cavalry units and for hauling heavy guns and equipment to the front. The British, French, and Canadian armies all had purchasing agents in Canada who scoured the country looking for cavalry remounts and artillery horses. As the British Columbia Interior had large numbers of wild horses, quite a market developed for those who could catch, break, and train horses. All the army required was for a horse to be ridden two or three times to be considered gentle enough for the troops. Returning soldiers were heard to remark, "Those darned remounts killed or wounded more men than did the German army."

John Roper Hull's Edith Lake Ranch, south of Kamloops, supplied a large number of horses to the military. The same applied to Joe Bulman's Willow Ranch, which became a centre for breaking and training remounts. With the shortage of good manpower available, a man who was tough enough to break horses day in and day out was worth a lot. One of these men was Bill Arnold, who arrived in the Nicola Valley from Montana with his father early in the war. Arnold was a big, barrel-chested man who had worked with horses since he was a youngster. He was already about forty-four years-old when he arrived but soon gained a reputation as a man who could ride "anything that wore hide." He went to work at the Willow Ranch, halter breaking and "sacking out" the wild horses that had been captured in the nearby hill country. He then turned them over to several young "bronc twisters," who did most of the riding. If they ran into a real tough horse, Bill would hop on and ride it to a standstill.

In that area, there were quite a few locally famous bucking horses. One of them was particularly mean and had the bad habit of rearing up and falling over backward, trapping the rider beneath several hundred pounds of horse with the saddle horn or cantle right in the rider's chest or stomach. The owner of the horse bet a hundred dollars to any takers that the horse could not be ridden. Bill Arnold, always up for the challenge, took him up on the bet.

Once word got around that Bill was going to ride the beast, quite a crowd assembled to watch the fun. The horse was saddled and the cinch pulled up tight and, true to form, humped its back and puffed up like a bullfrog. Before he got into the saddle, Bill took his heavy, shot-loaded quirt by the lash end and, as he hit the saddle, swung the quirt down as hard as he could between the horse's ears. The horse, stunned by the blow, dropped to its knees and then jumped up and took off at a dead run without as much as a buck. After a mad dash to the end of the pasture, Bill managed to bring him to a halt, then turned him and ran him back to the waiting crowd. By then the horse was tired out and slowed to a walk. Bill grinned and said, "Seems like he forgot to buck." He collected his hundred dollars and headed home.

<<< **9** >>>

Ranch Women

Eliza Swalwell, Cowgirl

IN THE EARLY DAYS OF the British Columbia Interior, it was a common practice for ranchers to marry Indigenous women. Until the coming of the railway in 1885, these families formed the majority of the population and were generally accepted by all.

George William Simpson was born in 1823 in Philadelphia of Scottish Presbyterian parents. In his mid-twenties, George was intrigued by the lure of California gold and travelled across the continent to try his hand at gold mining. He was unsuccessful there and, hearing of gold being discovered in the new British Colony of British Columbia, he headed north to try his luck in 1859. For a time he worked for the Harper brothers, driving cattle from Oregon to the goldfields but, by 1867, he was in the Okanagan Valley, where he eventually raised purebred beef cattle on what was called the Simpson Ranch.

Around 1870, Simpson married an Okanagan woman, Sarah, and they had three children. The eldest, Eliza Jane, married William Swalwell and later looked back on her early life in an account published in the Okanagan Historical Society's Eighth Report entitled "Girlhood Days in the Okanagan." She wrote how the children of the Indigenous women and non-Indigenous men, living far from the cities at a time when only the occasional stranger would pass by, enjoyed a life of freedom and a closeness to nature that they would remember with fondness in later years. Eliza's reminiscences are recorded in Chapter 3 of this book.

Elizabeth Greenhow, Lady Rancher

AFTER THE DEATH OF HER husband, Thomas Greenhow, in 1889, Elizabeth Greenhow was determined to carry on with the operation of the ranch. In the male-dominated society of the 1890s, she had to struggle to establish herself as a serious woman of business. Her first test came in 1892, when she took the Shuswap and Okanagan Railway to court and filed for arbitration as the railway (along the east side of Swan Lake) cut off 38.7 acres of her land. After a prolonged battle, she settled for seventy-five dollars an acre. This case served notice to all local businessmen that Elizabeth Greenhow was not a woman to be trifled with.

With this challenge out of the way, Elizabeth looked at fulfilling her long-time dream to build a suitable house in which to raise her children. She commissioned an architect, G.W. Grant of New Westminster to design a three-story Queen-Anne style mansion, described by the *Vernon News* as "one of the finest (if not the finest) in the upper country." The completed mansion had a fireplace in every room and cost in the range of ten thousand dollars, a fortune in those days. The lovely home, situated about fifty-five yards from the attractive O'Keefe mansion, built in 1886, did little to lessen the competitive feelings between Elizabeth and her uncle, Cornelius O'Keefe.

In 1894, Elizabeth, in partnership with Vernon's first settler, Luc Girouard, subdivided some of her property on the north edge of Vernon into half-acre lots. The following year, Luc Girouard passed away and his brother, Theo Girouard, negotiated a settlement with Elizabeth. The local paper reported, "Mr. Girouard desires us to state that though he has always found it a matter of difficulty to do business with a lady, in this case he was met in a most liberal and businesslike manner."

Elizabeth, along with Mary Ann O'Keefe and such notable women as Lady Aberdeen, was one of the driving forces behind the establishment of the Vernon Jubilee Hospital in 1897. She even offered free property on which to build the hospital, but her land was considered too far from town. After construction of the hospital, she was a frequent donor of financial assistance and farm produce to the project and, for a time, served as one of the directors of the hospital.

By the early 1900s, land around Vernon was in great demand for subdivision into orchards. After holding out for some time as prices escalated, Elizabeth and Cornelius O'Keefe sold off the majority of their vast holdings to the Land and Agricultural Company of Canada. This transaction netted Elizabeth $315,000, a fortune in a day when labourers made a dollar a day, and ensured that Elizabeth would have financial stability for the rest of her life.

A devoted mother to her two children, Thomas Junior and Mary Victoria, Elizabeth had them placed in a Catholic boarding school in California for their education. Her frequent trips to visit them convinced her that California would be a wonderful place to retire. In 1926, she left her beloved mansion and retired to sunny California to finish out her days. She died in 1941 at the age of eighty-seven.

<<< **10** >>>

Top Hands

Antoine Allen

ANTOINE ALLEN WAS ONE OF the first and the last of the old-time cowboys in British Columbia. He was born in 1855, in the Willamette River Valley in Oregon Territory, the son of a white miner and his Indigenous wife. In 1864, he travelled with Jerome and Thaddeus Harper on one of their cattle drives to British Columbia and remained with them for many years afterward. They taught him the cattle trade, and he worked for them on their ranches west of Kamloops and in the Cariboo.

Allen was one of the drovers on the drive that Thaddeus Harper organized to relieve the range of an overabundance of cattle. The drive started in May in the Dog Creek and Alkali Lake areas and worked its way to Kamloops and through the Okanagan to the United States. The cattle were driven across the border at Osoyoos Lake and then were forced to swim the Columbia River at the mouth of the Okanagan. From there the drive proceeded south through the Grand Coulee and crossed the Snake River near Fort Walla Walla. By then the drive had been going for almost seven months, and Newman Squires, who was in charge of the drive for Thaddeus Harper, decided to winter the cattle. Only a few men remained to winter-herd the cattle, and Allen returned to British Columbia with many of the other cowboys.

Antoine Allen remained in the Kamloops area. In 1881, he was working for James Todd on the South Thompson River east of Kamloops, and some years later appears to have worked for Thaddeus Harper on the Gang Ranch.

In 1910, the now-married fifty-five-year-old Allen took part in another major cattle drive. Ulysses Campbell, son of rancher Lewis Campbell, recruited him in Kamloops to be one of the head cowboys in a drive to supply beef to the construction camps of the Grand Trunk Pacific and Pacific Great Eastern Railways (now the BC Railway). Pat Burns held the contract and, after an experimental drive from the Chilcotin to Hazelton led by Joe Paine had proven successful, Burns had contracted Ulysses Campbell to take a series of drives north. Allen and the other cowboys took the train to Ashcroft to collect the saddle and pack horses that Burns had sent from Alberta. The cowboys spent a couple of weeks gathering cattle from all over the Chilcotin and assembled a herd of 800 steers at Riske Creek. The steers were carefully inspected and 300 of them culled from the herd. On May 10, the drive of 500 picked steers left the Chilcotin. It took eight days to reach Quesnel. They then battled through another 500 miles of brush and mud holes to reach Hazelton where Burns and Company had a slaughterhouse. That year, Allen accompanied another three drives of cattle, taking a total of 2,000 head to Hazelton. He remained involved in the drives until 1913, when a total of 12,000 head of Chilcotin cattle reached market.

He retired on a wave of success and lived in the Kamloops area near his three daughters until his death in 1936. Allen was one of the true pioneer cowboys who saw the cattle industry grow and change in the interior of British Columbia. He was voted into the BC Cowboy Hall of Fame in 2005 in the "Working Cowboy" category.

John (Hans) Richter

HANS RICHTER WAS BORN IN 1878, the fifth and youngest son of Francis Xavier "Frank" Richter, pioneer cattleman of the Similkameen Valley, and his Similkameen wife, Lucy. All the Richter sons were born at the "R" Ranch, which Frank sold to R.L. Cawston in 1884, moving his family to the Lower Ranch in what came to be known as Richter Pass. Hans was sent to school at the Okanagan Mission (later Kelowna) and boarded with the family of early settler Frederick Brent, returning home in the summer months to help with the ranch work. In 1892, Hans began attending the newly constructed school in the Similkameen Valley, even though it entailed a nine-mile ride in each direction. It was, perhaps, on these long daily rides that Hans developed his love of horses. As he grew older, he enjoyed working with horses and, when the first rodeos were held in the southern interior of British Columbia, he was an avid participant, winning many trophies, buckles, and medals.

Rodeo was in its infancy. There were few rodeo grounds, so people would park their wagons or vehicles in a circle to form a makeshift arena. Bucking horses would be snubbed to a post, blindfolded, and then saddled. The rider would mount, the blindfold would be removed, and the horse was untied. Then the fun would begin. In those days, bucking horses would be ridden until they stopped bucking, so rides often lasted for many minutes. They were not the eight-second rides of today. When the horse had been ridden to a standstill, the pickup man would ride alongside and help the rider dismount. A good pickup man was essential and Hans was acclaimed as one of the best pickup men and ropers on the rodeo circuit.

It was only natural that Hans should begin to raise his own bucking string from the wild horses he captured in the areas adjoining Richter Pass. He eventually owned a string of forty or more bucking horses that he would supply to rodeos in Vernon, Kelowna, Penticton, Grand Forks, and Christina Lake. Hans often trailed his bucking horses over the Dewdney Trail to rodeos in Chilliwack and Sumas and into Washington State. He even did the announcing at the rodeos, using a megaphone as he rode through the arena.

Hans was particularly proud that he once put on a rodeo in Victoria. He drove his horses over the trail to Hope and loaded them on boxcars bound for Vancouver. From there, they were put on barges and towed to Vancouver Island, where they entertained the people of Victoria and its surrounding area.

Hans married Sarah Marsel, the daughter of Similkameen stagecoach driver Peter Marsel. Sarah was some thirty years younger than Hans, who was in his fifties when they wed. Coincidentally, a few years earlier, Sarah's mother, Julia, had married Hans's older brother, Charlie Richter, after the death of Peter Marsel. Hans and Sarah had four sons and six daughters. Hans continued to supply the rodeo circuit with bucking stock well into the 1940s, working the Princeton and Kelowna rodeos until he was sixty years old. He died at the age of eighty-four in 1961 and was followed by Sarah the next year.

Jim Bonner: One Tough Cowboy

THE COWBOY HAS HAD A reputation for toughness since the beginning of the cattle industry in North America. Anyone who spends his life in the outdoors far from the niceties of civilization needs to be prepared for hardship, and the cowboy epitomizes the image of the rugged individual. But, even among those who lived this reputation for toughness, there were those who stood out from the rest. They were men and women who knew hardship and isolation and rose above them to not only persevere but to excel in the life that many would find impossibly difficult. Jim Bonner was one of these.

In the course of tending cattle, accidents have been known to happen, and sometimes it was hours before someone could be found to bandage up a cut or set a bone. So cowboys had to learn to "grin and bear it" if they were in pain. However, Jim Bonner's experience went far beyond the grin-and-bear stage.

Bonner worked for Dick Church on his Big Creek Ranch in the heart of the Chilcotin. Late in the fall of 1942, he was gathering up stray cattle in the Hungry Valley, an isolated valley high up in the foothills of the Coast Range. Bonner had been joined by Jimmy Rosette, who was looking for Gang Ranch cattle in the remote area. As the two cowboys combed the steep hillsides of the valley, Bonner's horse slipped on a frost-covered side hill and fell on him. His leg was shattered between the knee and ankle. There was no way out except by horseback. So Rosette helped him back into the saddle and, with the broken leg not even splinted, the two men rode twelve miles down to Fosbery Meadow, where there was a cabin. The cowboys spent the night at the cabin, and Rosette was able to fashion a makeshift splint. Once again, Bonner was helped into the saddle for another twelve-mile ride through swamp and jack pine to Gus Piltz's Sky Ranch, situated at an elevation of five thousand feet. By now the pain must have been unbearable but Bonner, whitefaced and grim, kept silent. From the Sky Ranch, Bonner travelled in the back of Piltz's pickup truck over a rough road to the Church Ranch at Big Creek, still far from civilization. The ordeal was far from over. At Big Creek, Bonner was loaded into the back of a car, which proceeded toward Williams Lake. But the combination of rain and snow made the road almost impassable, and the going was extremely slow. The seventy-five-mile trip to Williams Lake took nine hours! After three incredibly painful days and nights, Bonner arrived at the hospital, where the broken bones were set. Through the whole process, Bonner had kept quiet and uncomplaining.

"Roaring Bill"

JOE COUTLEE WAS THE SON of Alexander Coutlie (note the original spelling), a French Canadian from Trois-Rivières who had settled in the Nicola Valley in 1873 and married an Indigenous woman. At the age of ten, young Joseph's first real job was working cattle for Joseph Castillion, the Mexican packer who was one of the original settlers in the Nicola Valley. Joe came to work at the Douglas Lake Cattle Ranch at the age of twenty-three in 1892, under cow boss Joe Payne and stayed there for the next fifty-three years. Coutlee learned the cattle trade well under the sharp eye of Joe Payne and, when Payne left in 1896, Coutlee took over as cowboss of the Douglas Lake Cattle Ranch, a position that he was to hold until his death in 1944.

Coutlee had an incredible ability to read the range. He could eye up a field and accurately predict just how many head of cattle could graze that field and for how long. This ability allowed him to carefully manage the precious bunchgrass resource that sustained the Douglas Lake cattle. He always separated the herd and moved each group to the higher elevations in the summer so that no one range was overgrazed. Coutlee knew his stock as if they were his children, even when the Douglas Lake was running thirteen thousand head of mixed Shorthorn and Hereford. He could remember which cows had been pulled out of mud holes two years before and where certain calves were born.

Coutlee was a large man, over two hundred pounds and close to six feet tall. His cowboys referred to him as "Roaring Bill," and when he was crossed, he lived up to his nickname. He expected his twenty-odd cowboys to ride any horse they were given, break, shoe, and care for it, and repair its tack, not to mention rope cattle, repair fence, and cook for themselves if required. Many a cowboy was sent packing who failed to live up to Coutlee's expectations.

Coutlee married an Indigenous woman, Mary Ann Horne, who he affectionately nicknamed "Muggins." The two had a stormy relationship, especially when Joe was on a drinking spree when the work was all done, but Muggins stayed with him all his life and cared for their six children. She predeceased him, and when Joe died in 1945, he was buried alongside her in the Indigenous cemetery at Shulus, close to his childhood home. His legacy to the Douglas Lake Ranch was expressed by his long-time boss, Frank Ward:

> With all his failings he was a tower of strength to me especially in my early days, and I thank God he lived through my reign at Douglas Lake

for he made it that much more simple ... enabled me to get away from time to time and know that the cattle at any rate would be properly looked after. I never went off for a long voyage without having old Joe promise me he would not get off on a drunk during my absence, and to my knowledge he never did.

The Big Kid

JIM MADDEN APPEARED IN THE Nicola Valley during the 1890s and, from the thick Scottish burr in his speech, must have originated from the Scottish Highlands or Hebrides Islands. When in his cups, he was known to mutter about great catches of fish, which led one to believe that he had been a fisherman in his earlier days. But, true to the unwritten code of the ranching country, no one ever asked about his past, and he seemed to prefer it that way. His exuberant personality and childish innocence soon resulted in his being everywhere known by the nickname "the Big Kid." The simplicity of his lifestyle and his colourful adventures soon made him legendary in the Nicola and surrounding valleys.

He was a large man, over six feet in height and a full-bodied 240 pounds. In size and sheer physical presence, he was everything that a cowboy dreamed of being. But the resemblance to the typical cowhand stopped there. His shaggy hair was shoulder length and seemed to continue via his long beard to his woolly chest, creating one continuous mat of hair. His clothing was equally distinct, with his only concession to standard dress being an ancient flop-brimmed hat, stained and worn with the sweat and dirt of many days' hard work. The rest of his attire consisted of a plaid wool shirt and heavy wool pants stuffed into a pair of lace-up boots. Even in the most frigid weather, his clothes remained unchanged. Only the degree to which the shirt and boots were done up, ranging from wide open in the height of summer to fully closed in winter's coldest months gave any hint that the changing of the seasons affected him at all.

An independent spirit, the Big Kid chose to work by contract for the ranches in the area. During round-up and branding, he could ride and rope with the best of them, but he most often chose jobs that he could perform on his own, preferring to live alone. Fencing, land clearing, wood cutting, and occasionally winter feeding numbered among his favourite tasks. It was while putting up a log fence for the Douglas Lake Ranch that the Big Kid found himself in a jam that any other man might have considered disastrous. The logs were pine and oozing with pitch from the hot spring weather. As the Big Kid worked alone, he had to wrestle the logs into place and soon found the work hot and sweaty. He had to remove his shirt and open his woolly chest to the spring air to keep cool. But, as the pitch in the logs began to accumulate on his chest, he found that eventually his beard became glued in place, keeping his head in a permanently stooped position. Undeterred, he continued the job until, at the end of the day, he appeared at the ranch headquarters with his beard welded to his chest. It took the extensive application of kerosene and the careful manipulation of horse clippers for the Big Kid to manage to tilt his head far enough back to take a drink directly from a bottle.

During his time in the Nicola Valley, the Big Kid lived in two different cabins. The first and more permanent of these, referred to as "the Boar's Nest" for reasons that any visitor would find obvious, was on the Douglas Lake Ranch alongside a field that is still known as the Boar's Nest. The Big Kid's building techniques were as unique as his appearance. He selected building logs for their proximity to his cabin site rather than their straightness. This resulted in a series of large holes between the logs that were too large to fill with the conventional mud and straw chinking. But the Big Kid was undeterred. He collected a variety of empty liquor bottles from behind the local watering hole, the Quilchena Hotel, and used them to fill the largest holes. This successfully filled the cracks and also allowed daylight in without the need for windows. The end result created an interior like that of a medieval cathedral with sunlight filtering through stained-glass windows. The

Boar's Nest remained the Big Kid's bachelor home for many years and, like many bachelors, his dietary preferences and sanitary standards were dubious at best. Most often, boiled beans or boiled whole wheat were both the main course and dessert, but more exciting fare could occasionally made its way onto his rude table.

Such was the case on the day the local minister, showing a zeal for visiting the poor and needy, chose to drop by the Boar's Nest. The Big Kid's welcome was genuinely warm and friendly. He extended an invitation to the reverend to stay for lunch, which, the man of the cloth could see, consisted of a pot of beans boiling on the stove. The minister, undeterred by the fact that the Big Kid's shirt was off and his furry chest exposed, readily agreed. As they exchanged news and discussed their views on local events, the Big Kid explained that he was suffering from a cold that he could not shake. In the course of conversation, he seemed to be paying extremely close attention to a chunk of pork fat that was boiling along with the beans. He checked it regularly to see if it was done and, sometime before lunchtime, he fished it out of the pot and plunked it on his plate. The minister was struck by the particular attention that the Big Kid was paying to this chunk of pork. From time to time, he would touch it gently and turn it over carefully. Finally, at what he must have deemed the right moment, he seized the chunk of pork and, explaining the beneficial properties of hot pork grease, rubbed the chunk all over his massive hairy chest. Then, much to the minister's surprise, he carefully dropped the chunk back into the bean pot to reheat for lunch. History did not record the minister's reaction to this versatile chunk of pork in his lunch but, mindful of the obvious hospitality extended to him, he proceeded to eat lunch, watching carefully for curly chest hairs.

The Big Kid built his second cabin when he was working on an extended contract clearing a field along Quilchena Creek for the Triangle Ranch. The field is known to this day as the Big Kid Field, in many ways a monument to this industrious and colourful character. Somewhere around the turn of the century, the Big Kid spent a winter in this cabin and suffered severely frostbitten toes. The locals puzzled over how a man could suffer frostbite while sleeping in his own cabin, but the explanation eventually came to light. It seemed that the Big Kid was not lavish in his sleeping arrangements. He preferred to crawl between two cow hides rather than waste his hard-earned money on wool blankets. Apparently, during a particularly bitter winter night, the cow hides, not known for their square dimensions, slipped out of place. The Big Kid, preferring to keep his head warm as opposed to his feet, left his feet uncovered, and the result was disastrous.

This cabin was also the setting of another of the Big Kid's gourmet escapades. Once again, a visitor had dropped by and been generously invited for lunch. The Big Kid hinted that there was something special cooking on the stove, but the visitor felt somewhat dismayed when he spotted a long black tail, which bore a suspicious resemblance to that of a muskrat, protruding from the pot. Sure enough, when lunchtime arrived, the Big Kid pulled from the pot a muskrat, complete with hide, guts, feet, and eyes. Then, before the visitor's astonished eyes, he stripped the skin off and placed the cooked carcass on a plate. Carefully spooning out wheat that had been boiled in the same pot, he dug in with relish. Once again, we have no record of the visitor's reaction, but we can assume that he hardly did justice to this lunchtime feast.

The Big Kid spent the years around the First World War as a hand at the Guichon Ranch, still preferring to live alone in his own log cabin. By that time, he had accumulated enough worldly possessions to fill a cowhide trunk but, despite his impoverished appearance, the Big Kid was far from broke. He once complained to Lawrence Guichon about missing six hundred dollars in cash. The Big Kid was a supporter of the Red Cross and had recently been badgering Guichon to donate. Guichon got the Kid to promise that, if he could find the money, 10 percent of it would go to the Red Cross. Sure enough, Guichon found it under an old cup without a handle, lying upside down on the floor of the Big Kid's cabin. True to his word, the Big Kid donated sixty dollars to this worthwhile cause.

The Big Kid stayed in the Nicola Valley for close to thirty years, living in semi-retirement at the Guichon Ranch into the 1920s. But, sad to say, his story does not end happily. Toward the end of his days, a long-lost brother showed up and convinced him to invest his life savings in a sawmill near Princeton, BC. The sawmill venture failed, and the Big Kid lost everything. He died in New Westminster in 1948 at the ripe old age of seventy-seven.

Joe Payne

AMONG THE WORKING COWBOYS OF British Columbia, the pinnacle of success is the position of cow boss of the Douglas Lake Cattle Ranch, the largest ranch in Canada. Only a handful of men have held that position in the 130 odd years that the ranch has been in existence. Needless to say, the man who holds that job has to be among the best of his profession. This distinction goes back to the first cow boss at the Douglas Lake Ranch.

When J.B. Greaves was setting up the Douglas Lake Cattle Ranch in the early 1880s, he realized he needed a top-notch cow boss to tend the cattle while he looked after the business end of things. He was fortunate to hire Joe Payne, an American with rich and varied experience in handling cattle.

Payne proved to be a natural at handling cattle and men. Under his management, the Douglas Lake herd thrived, and the cowboys who worked for him developed into an efficient crew. The Indigenous cowboys worked particularly well with Payne, who had the patience to show them the preferred methods of handling cattle. He conscientiously divided his huge herd into small groups and moved them carefully throughout the year to avoid overgrazing of the precious bunchgrass. His techniques for getting cattle out of the bush, driving, sorting and holding cattle for market, and weaning became standard practice for decades to come. Payne was also an excellent veterinarian and, under his care, few cattle were lost in calving or to sickness.

Payne remained as cow boss for about ten years. In the 1890s, he left the Douglas Lake Ranch and went to work as a cattle buyer for Malcolm

McInnes, a former Nicola Valley cattleman, who, in partnership with Pat Burns, was supplying huge amounts of beef to the mining centres of the Kootenays. In 1897, when the Klondike gold rush started, Payne rounded up cattle from the BC Interior for Burns and Company and assembled them at the Gang Ranch. From there they were driven to Ashcroft and shipped by rail to the coast and by barge up to Skagway. Payne and his cowboys then drove the cattle over the White Pass and overland forty miles to Lake Bennett. There the cattle were loaded on scows to be shipped across Lake Bennett, then through a series of lakes and rivers to the Yukon River where they travelled an additional 200 miles to Dawson. The cattle sold at Dawson for a dollar a pound, or $800 to $1000 per head alive. This was the first of a succession of cattle drives that Burns and Company organized to the Klondike from the BC interior.

In 1911, Burns sent Payne to Mexico to check out land for possible purchase to add to Burns's expanding empire. This was not a simple mission. Payne had to remain inconspicuous and not reveal that the millionaire Burns was behind the purchase. As well, the political situation in Mexico was far from stable, with revolutionaries like Pancho Villa leading the opposition to the government. Never the most respectable-looking person at the best of times, Payne was arrested by the Mexican authorities and put in jail. It was some time before Burns and Company, working with the Canadian government, could convince the Mexican authorities that Payne's activities were legitimate.

During the First World War, Payne retired from the cattle business and went into partnership with Fred Bradley to operate the Brunswick Billiard Parlour on Victoria Street in Kamloops. But his restless nature and ill health soon prompted him to accept an offer from Dr. Vereerbrughen of Kamloops to go ranching in Argentina. From Argentina, he relocated to Brazil and finally, in 1924, he moved to California. He died there two years later, mourned by all the old-time cowboys who knew him as one of the best.

Val Haynes:
Last of the Old-Time Cowboys

VALENTINE CARMICHAEL HAYNES, THE ELDEST child of J.C. Haynes, the Collector of Customs at Osoyoos during the gold rush years, was the quintessential cowboy. By the time he was eight years old, he was cowboying with the best of the hands on his father's large ranch in the south Okanagan. In 1893, he went to work for Tom Ellis, who had acquired the vast Haynes family holdings and whose ranch headquarters were at present-day Penticton. When the Shatford brothers bought out Tom Ellis in 1905, Val became the foreman for the ranch and worked for them until they sold to the government in 1919.

Haynes rapidly gained a reputation as a cowboy among cowboys. His abilities were outstanding and, even though he never showed much interest in rodeos or competition, he was considered the best in roping in difficult places and under adverse conditions. He prided himself on his knowledge of cattle and often remarked that "I know all my cattle by the look on their faces." Despite being an excellent horseman, Haynes was never too fond of horses, knowing that the South Okanagan was home to thousands of wild horses that consumed large quantities of the precious bunchgrass resource, leaving less for his beloved cattle. In appearance, he was every inch a cowboy with his large, flat-brimmed Stetson, silk neckerchief, and woolly chaps.

Val Haynes acquired the Garrison Ranch and later the Swan Lake (Vaseux) Ranch and its range on Kruger Mountain. He married Elizabeth Runnels, whose mother was sister of Nespelem George, one of the most respected chiefs of the northwest. Haynes became one of the most respected ranchers in the Okanagan, never failing to help out one of the old-time cowboys, whether white or Indigenous, if he needed a hand. In all his years as a foreman and rancher, he always ate at the same table as his hired men and always referred to them as his cowboys, never his hired men. He was an excellent judge of cattle and horses and built his ranch up to be one of the finest in the province. His stock was always considered the best, and he never had to sell through the cattle auctions at Okanagan Falls—he shipped directly to the buyers and commanded top price.

Considered the last of the old-time cowboys, Haynes remained an active cowboy until a month before his death. It had been his habit for years to wean the calves on December 14, and on December 21, his birthday, he would drive the calves to Swan Lake Ranch. His last birthday, his eighty-seventh, was no exception and, with the help of his grandsons, he drove some two hundred calves about twenty miles. It could safely be said that his death in 1962 marked the end of an era in the history of ranching in British Columbia, an era that saw the lowly cattle drover capture the attention of the world and be transformed in the eyes of all who saw him into a figure of mythological proportions: the cowboy.

<<< **11** >>>

Mud Pups

B Y THE 1870S, THE BRITISH COMMONWEALTH had reached its zenith. Contemporary maps sported large splashes of red, lending truth to the maxim that "the sun never set on the British Empire." Great Britain's economy flourished as its empire grew and a large merchant class developed out of the wave of expanding trade and commerce. John Ruskin cried out to this merchant class in 1870 when he said: "There is a destiny now possible to us, the highest ever set before a nation to be accepted or refused ... This is what England must either do or perish; she must found colonies as fast and as far as she is able, formed of her most energetic and worthiest men; seizing every piece of fruitful waste ground she can set her foot on."

Ruskin's call to young men to go to the colonies and spread what was considered the "superior" culture of England did not go unheeded. For many middle-class families whose sons and daughters had received the best education Britain could offer, it was only appropriate that they emigrate to the colonies and establish "the light of civilization" there. The colonies offered a solution for parents who were looking for a suitable place for their energetic and, at times, unbridled younger sons. Not only would the boys' energies be put to good use in furthering the cause of

Empire, but there was every possibility that they could make a decent life there.

This heady call for England's "most energetic and worthiest men" did contain some intelligent and pragmatic forethought. Anxious parents recognized that their sons needed the maximum possible advantage in their new country and that this could be best assured by placing them under the care of someone already familiar with the customs and circumstances of the land. Many parents would contact someone of good reputation who was already established in the colony and arrange for the younger son to be placed in his care and custody until the son could make his own way. The families considered cattle ranching to be an honourable profession, and the ranches of British Columbia seemed perfect for the younger sons. Most often this involved paying the rancher for his time and trouble. And so, from the 1870s on, there was an influx of well-educated and energetic young men who came at their parents' expense and stayed to make a life for themselves.

In the interior of British Columbia, these apprentice ranchers were called "mud pups," a term that initially expressed disdain from the "real cowboys" who had paid, and continued to pay, their own way through life. However, so many mud pups stayed on and became hard-working cowboys and successful ranchers that the term lost its negative ring and eventually indicated someone who had arrived under favourable circumstances but who worked as hard as everyone else to make a go of things.

A typical mud pup who came to learn the ranching business and stayed was Robert Cecil Cotton, who came from Hampton Court, England, to the M.G. Drummond Ranch in the Chilcotin in 1897. After a year and a summer with no pay, he began to earn the grand sum of twenty-five dollars a month during the winter of 1898. Like many mud pups, after learning the trade, Cotton returned to England, where he obtained enough money to buy the ranch from Drummond and rename it the Cotton Ranch. He operated it until his death in 1954.

Hugh Bayliff

HUGH PEEL LANE BAYLIFF'S ANCESTORS included the Peels, who produced two prime ministers of Britain, and the Lane family, who were mayors of Hereford. Bayliff came as an eighteen-year-old to British Columbia in 1882 and presented himself to Clement Cornwall at Ashcroft Manor. Cornwall arranged for Bayliff to work for William Roper at Cherry Creek, west of Kamloops, to learn the ranching business. Bayliff later reported that he worked feeding cattle every day from early December until March 9 before he earned any time off—a Sunday afternoon. During that winter, he wrote home: "We are all much too big. I am so tall, in cold weather the ends of me are so far away from the centre of warmth ... I am getting so horribly mean and miserly ... I hope mother will send me some socks. I try to hide the fact that mine are worn out."

The young mud pup learned his trade well and distinguished himself with his roping skills. He also became an excellent rider and was often called upon to break a cayuse that no one else could handle. William Roper was one of the first to attempt to improve his stock, importing Hereford cattle and Clydesdale horses, and Bayliff saw the advantages of purebred stock before most ranchers even thought about it. Before long, he became Roper's cow boss and took charge of driving cattle to the CPR construction camps.

A severe drought hit the interior of British Columbia in the summer of 1886 and Bayliff, thinking it was time to start a ranch of his own, set out to find a place with good grass and water. His travels brought him to the Chilcotin plateau, which at that time was still sparsely settled. Bayliff took a job looking after a pack train for Tom Hance and took his time to check out the country. He spent that winter in a little cabin overlooking the Chilcotin River. In the spring, he was impressed with the way the Chilcotin River overflowed its banks and naturally irrigated the bottomland. Remembering the dry Cherry Creek summers, he pre-empted a beautiful piece of land between Alexis Creek and Redstone and went into partnership with another Englishman, Norman Lee.

To stock his ranch, he went to William Roper and made an arrangement that showed the trust that had grown between to the two men. He took 100 yearling heifers with the understanding that, in five years, the partners would return the original 100 plus one half of the cattle they would produce. Some Shuswap cowboys from the Kamloops area helped drive the heifers and a few purebred Hereford bulls to the new ranch. However, after crossing the Fraser River at the Gang Ranch, the Shuswaps would come no farther, as they were afraid of the warlike Chilcotins. They roped and banded all the heifers, and Bayliff continued alone. True to his word, Bayliff made good his agreement, returning over 200 cows to Roper five years later.

In 1891, Bayliff returned to England and brought back enough funds to purchase Norman Lee's share of the ranch. He also brought back a bride, Gertrude Tyndle, a daughter of the editor of *The London Times*. Mrs. Bayliff was a skilled sidesaddle rider and regularly helped with round-ups. She also owned two racehorses and entered them in races at Becher's Prairie at Riske Creek.

The Bayliffs stayed true to their upbringing, always dressing for dinner at a table set with silver and fine china. They were also enthusiastic polo players and organized games among the local settlers. When Hugh Bayliff died in 1934, his holdings, the 3000-acre Chilanko Ranch, were taken over by his son, Gay. The Chilanko Ranch is operated by the Bayliff family to this day.

Coutts Marjoribanks

ONE OF THE TRULY COLOURFUL characters in the Okanagan Valley in the 1890s was Coutts Marjoribanks (pronounced "march-banks"). The younger son of the aristocratic Marjoribanks family, Coutts was educated in the best British schools but showed no inclination to pursue an academic career. In fact, Coutts Marjoribanks had a boisterous and outgoing nature and a decided tendency to outdoor activity. Although the aristocratic upper class could indulge their love of the outdoors in the socially acceptable joy of the chase, this did not seem to be enough for Coutts. His family decided when he was still very young that he was destined "for the colonies" to join the other overly energetic younger sons of England's best families who had gone before him. So it was that, in the mid-1880s, Coutts was placed in the care of the owners of the Horseshoe Ranch in North Dakota (the United States was considered a step below but part of the Empire nonetheless). The western ranching way of life was just what he needed to bring him into his own. He took to cowboying like a duck to water, and relished the rough-and-ready lifestyle that sneered at the more placid approaches to accomplishing things. His skills in riding, roping, and handling cattle grew, but his family regarded his lifestyle as far from acceptable. As his niece, Lady Pentland, put it, "Coutts was not prospering there."

The answer to the dilemma that Coutts posed to his family seemed near at hand. His older sister, Ishbel Maria Marjoribanks, had married Lord Aberdeen and so become Lady Aberdeen. Lord and Lady Aberdeen, enthralled by the Canadian West, particularly the Okanagan Valley, purchased the 13,261-acre Coldstream Ranch near Vernon in 1891. To the Marjoribanks family it seemed opportune, as there was one family member with experience in looking after a large ranch: Coutts Marjoribanks. History has recorded that Lady Aberdeen was the dominant partner in her marriage and, in this case as in many others, her will prevailed. Coutts was installed as the manager of the Coldstream Ranch.

Coutts Marjoribanks's tenure at the Coldstream was not a happy one—at least not for the owners. He really preferred the daily activities of cowboying to the paperwork of management. His true love was the cowboy lifestyle, which he lived with all the passion and recklessness he could muster. The famous Canadian poet Charles Mair described Coutts in a letter written from the Okanagan in 1892: "Lord Aberdeen's large ranches are here, looked after by his brother-in-law, Marjoribanks—a rum stick who goes about dressed like a cowboy, and indulges freely in Scotch whisky. Not a bad chap though with all his horseplay, and antics." Like most who met Coutts during this time, however, Mair could not resist his flamboyant personality and admitted begrudgingly to liking the character.

When Coutts first arrived at the Coldstream, one of the local wags insisted on pronouncing his surname as "major-eye-banks" with the accent on the middle syllable. This was soon shortened to "Major" and before too long the stories of "Major's" exploits became legend in the Okanagan. He was notorious for riding his horse into the Kalamalka Hotel bar when he wanted a drink, which was whenever he was in town. To his credit, this would have involved some good riding, as the steps to the hotel were steep. General opinion was that "his riding excelled his management of the ranch." In 1895, he "resigned" as manager of the Coldstream but stayed in the area, purchasing property and building a house in the Coldstream area. Living close to the ranch, he could always join in on the round-ups and the other activities that were most dear to his heart.

Mud Pup Robinson

THE MAJORITY OF "MUD PUPS" (younger sons of the British upper class sent to the colonies to learn ranching) thrived in the open ranges of the British Columbia Interior. But there were a few who made the most of being far from the discipline of home and took full advantage of regular payments from "daddy" to indulge in a life of leisure. One of these was Edward Robinson, who arrived at Thomas Wood's ranch in the Okanagan Valley in 1862. He was the son of successful businessman, George Robinson of St. John's, Newfoundland, and had no doubt enjoyed a pampered life until he was pushed from the nest to make his own way in life.

Edward Robinson was a mere seventeen years of age when he arrived at the Wood Ranch. Thomas Wood's first clue to potential problems with Edward was the fact that he had already been apprenticed to a rancher in the North-West Territories, in what is now present-day southern Alberta.

He had been dismissed from that position for reasons not determined, but it certainly had not been through a propensity for hard work. However, the offer was one that no struggling rancher could refuse. Thomas Wood was to receive the princely sum of a thousand dollars a year to teach Robinson the intricacies of cattle ranching. Robinson's father offered this amount to cover "instruction and keep" and also would pay "for damages done by his son."

Wood soon learned that Robinson was more interested in visiting other young men in the area and in roaming the Okanagan hills shooting game. The only exception to his prolonged truancy was a five-week period the next fall when Robinson helped with haying. For this he was paid fifty dollars, an amount that was well above the going rate at the time for labourers of a dollar a day.

Despite Robinson's obvious indifference to all things to do with ranching, in 1886, his father settled up with Thomas Wood for the first three years of "training" and asked him to purchase a ranch for his son and stock it with cattle. Wood obtained a ranch and placed three thousand dollars' worth of cattle on it for young Robinson to start out as a rancher. But he did not do this without grave misgivings about Robinson's ability to carry on the hard work of ranching. So Wood, a native of St. John's himself, travelled there to meet with George Robinson face to face. The father was undeterred and offered to cover all additional costs such as his son's use of Thomas Wood's horses and stable.

Not surprisingly, a combination of the hard winter of 1886–87 and Robinson's disregard of his cattle resulted in a complete loss of his herd. When his father heard of this, he paid Wood to restock the ranch. After another difficult winter reduced this second herd of cattle, it was realized by all concerned, even George Robinson, that Edward was not suited for ranching and had better sell off his herd and try some other form of employment.

As a parting gesture, Edward tried to charge Thomas Wood for seven years' wages that he thought he had coming. Wood's reaction is not recorded, but it is quite certain that Edward Wood left the Okanagan neither richer in cash or in wisdom.

Riding to Hounds

CLEMENT AND HENRY CORNWALL'S LINEAGE could be traced as far back as Richard I in the twelfth century. The Cornwalls pre-empted land on the Thompson River in 1862 and established a successful ranch and stopping house, building the core of Ashcroft Manor, which still stands to this day, in 1863. As Englishmen to the core, the brothers decided that one of their country's most exhilarating sports should be imported into the Colony of British Columbia. And what could be more English than riding to hounds? In 1868, they imported four foxhounds from their native Gloucestershire. One of the four died on the long trip around the Horn but the remaining three, Ringwood, Rapid, and Daisy, formed the nucleus of the famous Cornwall hounds.

The brothers' next problem was finding foxes to chase, for foxes in the interior of British Columbia are scarce indeed. But the Cornwalls were undeterred. In the absence of foxes, they would chase coyotes, which were plentiful, as well as larger and faster than foxes. With the problem of quarry resolved, the brothers had no problem persuading their neighbouring ranchers to join in the fun. Some even went to the expense of purchasing red coats to make the scene even more "a little bit of England."

The hunt would begin about ten in the morning and, if the neighbours were otherwise occupied, the party would only include Clement and Henry accompanied by an Indigenous cowboy named Harry. Often the hunt would last all day and, on one occasion, the exuberant huntsmen did not drag themselves home until one the following morning. Often, Harry, who had better hearing and eyesight than the brothers, would race ahead with the pack instead of staying behind to whip up the stragglers among the dogs. However, the Cornwalls were good sports and always spoke highly of him.

The hunts continued well into the 1880s. The November 25, 1886, Kamloops *Inland Sentinel* has an account of "Gov. Cornwall's Hounds" (Clement Cornwall was Lieutenant Governor of British Columbia by then) and describes a series of hunts with the Cornwall pack in the Nicola Valley.

With eleven men and five women, hounds, and horses all hosted by William Pooley, a hunt was held on Monday, Wednesday, and Friday. On each occasion, a coyote was scented and a merry chase took place. Happily for the coyote, the Nicola country has abundant heavy brush and rocky areas and, in each case, the coyote sought refuge in an inaccessible place. On the Monday, the entire pack of hounds disappeared into the heavy brush and was not recovered until the following day.

Sadly, the imported hounds failed to thrive in the Ashcroft country and were often quite sick. Perhaps inbreeding or nutritional deficiency contributed to their bad health. A rancher from Manitoba bought them and, as Clement Cornwall wrote in his diary, "the glory of Ashcroft departed." He followed this entry with a verse:

> *I have lived my life, I am nearly done,*
> *But I freely admit that the best of my fun*
> *I had to horse and hound.*

<<< **12** >>>

Famous Ranches

The Founding of O'Keefe Ranch

CORNELIUS O'KEEFE WAS THE SON of a dirt-poor Irish immigrant farmer who had settled in the Ottawa Valley. So when he first saw the bunchgrass ranges at the head of Okanagan Lake, he couldn't believe that the lush bottomland was available for homestead, or "pre-emption," as it was then called. He had been driving cattle up from the Willamette Valley in Oregon far to the south with his partner, Thomas Wood, when they met Thomas Greenhow from the north of England. The three men had pooled their meagre herd of cattle and drove them north across the Columbia River and into British territory.

It was the middle of June, 1867, and all three men were concerned that the market for fine Oregon cattle was dwindling, along with the supply of gold in the Cariboo region. They decided that the future lay in taking up their own land in this fertile corner of the Colony of British Columbia. So each man staked out a rough 160-acre plot of land; O'Keefe and Greenhow took property about a mile from the head of the lake straddling Meadow Creek (later to be called Deep Creek) and Thomas Wood staked his pre-emption a short distance down the west side of Okanagan Lake. Four years later, Wood was to move to the south end of a lake that came to be called

Wood Lake, but O'Keefe and Greenhow stayed on the land until they were buried on it, many years later.

The three were not the first to settle in the North Okanagan. In 1864, two brothers, Forbes George and Charles Vernon, and their friend Charles Houghton, took out military grants in the Coldstream Valley. Farther north, near present-day Enderby, A.L. Fortune settled in 1866.

O'Keefe seems to have been the dominant partner of the three. As early as 1868, a year after they had settled, a drover wrote about going to "O'Keefe's" to see about some cattle." Eventually, the O'Keefe Ranch became the entry point into the Okanagan Valley and early settlers began to refer to the location as "Okanagan." They would arrive by horseback on the trail from Fort Kamloops and then head north up the Spallumcheen Valley or south through the Okanagan in search of suitable homesteads. An 1881 map shows three settlements in the entire valley, Houghton (Coldstream Ranch), Okanagan Mission (later Kelowna), and Okanagan. Of course, cities such as Vernon, Kelowna, and Penticton were still in the future.

To cater to the gold miners and the growing number of settlers arriving in the area, Cornelius O'Keefe opened a small general store to provide necessary provisions and a place to exchange news. He would take a pack train to Fort Kamloops and purchase enough supplies to keep the little store going for a month or two and pack them back to his ranch. This was the first store to operate in the Okanagan Valley.

While there were several ranchers who settled ahead of Cornelius O'Keefe, his is the only ranch that was still being lived in by the original family a hundred years later. Today some of the oldest buildings in the Valley are still being used and preserved as part of the O'Keefe Ranch heritage site.

O'Keefe Ranch Post Office

CORNELIUS O'KEEFE WAS A MAN with a tremendous drive to make something of his life. Not content to just raise cattle, he was the first rancher in the North Okanagan to open a general store on his property. His ranch became a gathering point for newcomers to the Okanagan Valley and soon was being called "Okanagan." So it is no surprise that, once British Columbia had joined the Canadian Confederation in 1871, the man who rallied the few settlers in the area to ask the Canadian government for a post office was Cornelius O'Keefe. As a result of the petition organized by O'Keefe, the chief postal inspector announced in the *Victoria Colonist* on August 6, 1872, that he "had made temporary arrangements with Mr. Barnard for a weekly mail service to Kamloops and Okanagan." The very next day, the same newspaper had an advertisement from Barnard's Express:

> Barnard's Express Stages for Okanagan ... the undersigned has placed a line of Passenger Stages on the New Wagon Road to Okanagan, running in close connection with Stages from Yale to Barkerville ... A General Express Business will be transacted over the route. Freight carried, Parcels delivered, Communications executed, Collections made. F.J. Barnard & Co.

It is important to note that the name "Okanagan" referred to the area at the head of the lake settled by Cornelius O'Keefe and Thomas Greenhow on their land not far from the original Hudson's Bay Company Brigade Trail.

This first post office in the Okanagan Valley was established on August 14, 1872 with Cornelius O'Keefe as postmaster, a position that he held for the next forty years. The post office was located in the tiny little general store that O'Keefe had set up on his ranch. The "Okanagon" Post Office was so spelled because the clerk who recorded the new post office in Ottawa miscopied the form. It was not until 1904 that the name was corrected to Okanagan. Once the post office was established at the ranch, the BC Express Stage Lines ran a weekly stagecoach from Cache Creek to the O'Keefe Ranch on the new wagon road from Fort Kamloops. It carried all the mail and passengers to the O'Keefe Ranch and then turned around and headed back to

Cache Creek via Fort Kamloops. O'Keefe would put up stagecoach passengers for the night if necessary, before they proceeded on horseback to their destination in the Valley.

The stagecoach travelled to Okanagan once a week, leaving Cache Creek on Wednesday mornings at ten o'clock and returning the following week to connect with the stages going north and south on the Cariboo Wagon Road. Even though there was a post office established in Okanagan Mission, near present-day Kelowna, at the same time, there was no mail delivery that far south because there was no road beyond the O'Keefe Ranch. In 1876, construction began on a wagon road to Okanagan Mission, but for some years after the road was completed in 1877, mail was carried from the O'Keefe Ranch to Okanagan Mission on horseback.

Royalty Comes to the O'Keefe Ranch

IN 1882, THE OKANAGAN VALLEY was all abuzz. Queen Victoria's son-in-law was coming to visit! This was almost like having the Queen herself drop by for lunch. The Marquis (pronounced *mar' kwis* in the English way) of Lorne was Governor General of Canada at the time but, more importantly, he was married to Princess Louise, the Queen's daughter. He and his lovely wife, after whom Lake Louise in the Rockies was named, planned to come to British Columbia as part of their duties. The visit was to focus on the capital city of Victoria and the two other cities of consequence, New Westminster and Nanaimo, the future Vancouver being an insignificant community called Gastown at the time. But the Governor General and his party (unfortunately not including his illustrious wife) were to travel through the Interior to view the countryside and to allow the Marquis to indulge in one of his favourite activities, hunting.

So, in September 1882, the Governor General and his private secretary, Major de Winton, ex-Lieutenant Governor Joseph Trutch, and several others, made their way to the Okanagan via Ashcroft, Kamloops, and

Lambley's Landing (today's Enderby). From there, they travelled to the house of Cornelius O'Keefe at the head of Okanagan Lake. Vernon (or Priest's Valley, as it was then called) was little more than a few settlers and a hotel. The party stayed for three nights from October 8 to 11 in O'Keefe's log house, since his lovely mansion was still a thing of the future. Donald Graham, another Okanagan pioneer, later reminisced:

> When we heard of his visit, Donald Matheson and myself rode to O'Keefe's and met with the Marquis there. He sat on the end of a log and talked to us in a most friendly manner for half an hour or more. Mr. O'Keefe had been married for about a year, so it was not 'bachelor' cooking he got.

On Monday, Cornelius O'Keefe drove the Governor General by horse and wagon to the Coldstream Ranch, then owned by Forbes George Vernon who, along with his brother, Charles, had originally settled at the site of present-day Vernon in 1862. The party returned to O'Keefe's escorted by a large number of Okanagan people, all well mounted, from the reservation at the head of the lake. They spent all day Tuesday hunting the abundant game birds in the hills around the ranch. On Wednesday morning, before departing, the Marquis sat on a small hill across Deep Creek and drew a sketch of the O'Keefe Ranch and its setting, entitled "Vanguard of the Pine, near Okanagon [sic] Lake, Oct. 11, 1882." This wonderful memento is now in the Provincial Archives of BC, and a copy can be seen at the O'Keefe Ranch.

The BX Ranch

FRANCIS JONES BARNARD, THE FOUNDER of the North Okanagan's BX Ranch, was a true British Columbia pioneer. He started what was to become the longest stagecoach line in North America by carrying a huge sack of letters and papers on his back for a distance of 300 miles, entirely on foot. Barnard arrived in Victoria from his native Quebec City in 1859 at the beginning of the gold rush to the Cariboo. After trying various jobs in the new Colony of British Columbia, he took over an express business from a man named Jeffrey in 1861. Anxious to corner the contract to carry mail, he agreed to carry letters and papers on his back from Yale to Cariboo and return. This involved scrambling along the narrow trails of the Fraser Canyon before the construction of the Cariboo road.

The next year, Barnard started a "pony express", meaning that he led a horse loaded with letters and papers from Yale to Barkerville, and in July, landed the contract to carry Her Majesty's mail into the Interior. In 1864, Barnard placed a line of fourteen stagecoaches on the Cariboo Road, each carrying up to fourteen passengers and drawn by six horses. The company he established was called Barnard's Express and Stage Line, known to all simply as "the BX."

As his business grew, Barnard began to look for land where he could train and care for his stagecoach horses. He spotted the lush bunchgrass ranges of the North Okanagan and pre-empted 160 acres in 1872, the beginnings of the BX Ranch. To stock this ranch with the best of stagecoach horses, he sent one of his crack drivers, Steve Tingley, to southern California to purchase four hundred Morgan cross horses. Tingley drove these horses all the way back to the BX Ranch, where they were branded with the familiar BX brand. These horses were trained to pull stagecoaches and were not really "broken," so that they would average six miles an hour on level ground for about eighteen miles before they were changed. The horses were used on the main run from Yale to Barkerville, the longest stagecoach run in North America at the time, and for branch lines, including the run from Cache

Creek through Fort Kamloops, which terminated at the O'Keefe Ranch, the end of the wagon road into the Okanagan in the 1870s.

Barnard incorporated his business into the British Columbia Express Company in 1871 and sold 25 percent each to Steve Tingley and another expert driver, James Hamilton, but the name BX was still universally used. The BX Ranch was still owned by the Barnard family and used to raise horses, eventually being purchased by Alexander Macdonnell, who continued to use it as a horse ranch. But the advent of the motor car spelled the beginning of the end of horse-drawn transportation, and the BX Ranch became involved in mixed farming. Eventually, the land was subdivided and became the BX district, as it is now known. A remnant of the BX Ranch is still being farmed today.

J.B. Greaves

JOSEPH BLACKBOURNE GREAVES (PRONOUNCED "GRAVES") was born in Pudsey, England, and came to British Columbia in 1864. After successfully driving cattle from Oregon to the goldfields, he settled near Savona's ferry on the Thompson River (so-named by the English drovers' pronunciation of Francois Saveneau 's name). During the 1870s, when markets for cattle were few in British Columbia, Greaves regularly drove cattle down the Cariboo road to the head of steamboat navigation at Yale and then to the cities of New Westminster, Victoria, and Nanaimo. Victoria's *British Colonist* newspaper extolled the cattle as "fine specimens of that section of the mainland for stock raising."

But Greaves was looking for greater success. He watched with interest as the Canadian Pacific Railway was being constructed through the Fraser Canyon. Railway contractor Andrew Onderdonk employed five thousand men during the summer of 1881 and, to feed them, invited tenders for a large and steady supply of fresh beef for the work crews. Their requirements were so great that only the largest ranches could hope to answer their needs. Not surprisingly, Thaddeus Harper who, with his brother Jerome, had been a cattleman since the early gold rush years, won the contract. Harper sold off all his surplus cattle from his massive herds on the Gang Ranch and set about purchasing all the cattle he could from Cariboo and Chilcotin ranchers. Prices for cattle began to move upward to over twenty dollars a head, and the market for 1882 looked even more promising as railway construction reached its peak.

As the 1882 construction season approached, Greaves saw the potential for controlling the market. In December 1881, he contacted Benjamin Van Volkenburgh, who operated the British Columbia Meat Market in Victoria and had purchased cattle from the Harpers since 1880. Greaves convinced Van Volkenburgh that, for $80,000, he could purchase enough cattle to control the cattle market in British Columbia and guarantee obtaining the contract to supply beef to the CPR work crews for the next several years. Van Volkenburgh enlisted the support of some of the more wealthy British Columbians, including Joseph Pemberton, William Curtis Ward of the Bank of British Columbia, Charles W.R. Thomson of the Victoria Gas Company, and Judge Peter O'Reilly.

The new syndicate thus formed agreed to begin quietly purchasing all available cattle through the Thompson and Okanagan districts during the winter of 1881–82. Greaves, who was responsible for buying cattle, purchased 22,000 head in the Nicola Valley early in the new year at $20 to $23 per head. The cattle were purchased and held on the seller's ranches until they would be needed. Then Greaves headed for the Okanagan Valley where his helper, Brock McQueen, a former overlander, had already bought four hundred head at Okanagan Mission (later Kelowna). Greaves wrote to his partners of his intention to "get 30 or 35 Hundred Head of Cattle that will give our Compy [sic] control of the market for this season." It was a calculated gamble that could result in the syndicate holding thousands of head of cattle with nowhere to sell them.

Cornering the Market

J.B. GREAVES INTENDED TO CONTROL the cattle market and land the lucrative contract to supply beef to the thousands of railway construction workers in British Columbia in 1882. With the backing of a high-powered syndicate, he spent the winter of 1881-82 buying cattle in the Okanagan and Nicola Valleys.

At the same time, Thaddeus Harper of the Gang Ranch, characteristically optimistic that he would win the 1882 contract for CPR beef, was purchasing cattle in the Kamloops area and intending to buy in the Okanagan and Similkameen. It was not long before cattlemen realized that something was afoot. By April, the *British Columbian* newspaper had heard of the competition and wrote: "Corner in Beef: It is reported that some shrewd speculators have secured a corner in Mainland beef, and that in consequence meat will have an upward tendency. It is estimated that a cool $150,000 will be made out of the unfortunate consumers, unless the 'corner is broke' by some means not at present discovered." The price of marketable cattle climbed steadily, eventually reaching twenty-five dollars a head, and soon all three-year-old and older cattle that had been accumulating on the ranges had been sold.

Despite the efforts of J.B. Greaves and his partners, Thaddeus Harper received the contract to supply beef to the CPR for 1882. Undeterred, the syndicate continued to buy up cattle, still hoping to control the market. Harper successfully supplied beef during 1882 and obtained a renewed contract for 1883, but his supply of cattle could not meet the demands of the CPR work crews and, in the middle of the 1883 season, the syndicate finally took over the lucrative contract.

From the middle of the 1883 season until the end of railway construction, the syndicate controlled the market and prospered just as they had hoped. Greaves continued to travel through the Interior and purchase cattle well into the 1890s. Ranchers in the Okanagan, Thompson, and Nicola Valleys and those in the Cariboo came to trust that Greaves would pay fair prices and that his notes of credit were as good as cash. In the early years,

Greaves would simply confirm a deal with a handshake and leave the cattle to be picked up later.

It was soon obvious that the syndicate would need a ranch of its own to hold the cattle and raise them. Greaves formed a partnership with Charles M. Beak, who held a large amount of land in the Douglas Lake area. The next spring, Greaves, Beak, and syndicate members William Curtis Ward and Charles Thompson bought out the rest of the original syndicate members, who had already realized a huge profit. The four men then incorporated "a joint stock company ... for the purpose of carrying on a farming, stock raising and butchering business," the Douglas Lake Ranch. The ranch owned over 8,500 head of cattle and 8,000 acres of land. From this beginning, the Douglas Lake Ranch was to grow to be the largest cattle ranch in Canada.

Alfred Goodwin

ALFRED GOODWIN AND HIS BROTHER, Fred, pre-empted land near Fish Lake, northeast of the Douglas Lake Ranch, in 1891. Late that same year, the brothers acquired an additional three half-sections when the twenty-nine-square mile Marsh Meadows opened up for acquisition. This land bordered the Douglas Lake Ranch on the west and, right from the start, Douglas Lake manager J.B. Greaves and Alfred Goodwin were at odds.

Over the next few years, a number of incidents fuelled the animosity between the two. In 1904, Goodwin, in an attempt to increase his holdings, built a fence around a field that was Crown land. The fence was regularly broken down, especially when Douglas Lake cowboys were in the area. This did not help an already strained relationship and, in 1907, matters came to a dramatic head. Neighbouring rancher Billy Lauder was riding across Goodwin's land to purchase some cattle and noticed twenty-five head of horses, mostly Clydesdales, many with the distinctive 111 (one eleven) Douglas Lake Ranch brand on their shoulder blotched out. Lauder informed Greaves of what he had seen. Greaves sent long-time Douglas Lake cowboys Joe Coutlee and Jack Whiteford over to have a look and they found 23 horses, 13 of which had their brands disfigured. They drove the horses to the home ranch, and Greaves sent to Nicola for Constable Walter Clark. Clark conducted a search and found two more horses. Although it was obvious what had happened, there was no concrete proof that Goodwin had taken the horses or altered their brands, so a reward of $1,500 was offered to anyone who could help in the arrest and conviction of the horse thief. The provincial government offered a further $500.

Later that year, Oliver Walker, who had been in charge of Goodwin's cattle in 1907, confirmed that he had helped Goodwin steal the Douglas Lake horses and change their brands. Charges were then laid against Goodwin for stealing fourteen two-year old horses from the Douglas Lake Ranch and altering their brands. Further investigation saw a number of other charges laid against Alfred Goodwin.

The preliminary hearing in Kamloops uncovered much about Goodwin's dealings. Oliver Walker's evidence was the most damaging. He testified that he and Goodwin had rounded up twenty-five Douglas Lake horses and put fourteen of them into their corrals, where they treated the brands with Fleming's Lump Jaw Cure or Spavin Cure. These salves caused a blister on the hide that would slough off, taking the lump, or spavin, with it. They had the same effect on brands, removing them from the hide and leaving behind a sore that would heal over, leaving only scar tissue.

In the spring assizes in Vernon, Goodwin's lawyer, A.D. McIntyre, cleverly questioned Walker's reliability, suggesting that he was the mastermind behind the scheme and that his testimony was more for the reward money rather than any desire to see justice done. Goodwin himself took the stand and denied any involvement in the matter. McIntyre was so effective that the jury failed to reach a verdict, and a new trial was set for Kamloops. After hearing the same evidence, the jury returned a verdict of "not guilty," and Goodwin was released. Wisely, he decided not to return to his ranch, preferring to lease it out and move to the Monte Creek area, away from his arch-enemy, J.B. Greaves.

The Gang Ranch

THE HARPER BROTHERS, JEROME AND Thaddeus, began driving cattle into the Colony of British Columbia in 1860, from as far away as California. Initially, they grazed their cattle on land east of Fort Kamloops that became the Harper Ranch, before driving them on to the goldfields. As the gold frontier advanced into the fabled Cariboo country, the brothers began to purchase land closer to the mining region, eventually operating a slaughterhouse in Barkerville, the heart of the Cariboo goldfields.

For a time, in the early 1860s, the Harpers had held their cattle in the area north of Lillooet along the "River Trail" on the east side of the Fraser River in the area around Dog Creek. The vast stretches of grasslands across the Fraser probably caught their entrepreneurial eyes, but the inaccessibility of the area made them hesitate—cattle could only cross the Fraser River with great difficulty before reaching the main roads and trails on the way to the Cariboo market. The pragmatic brothers therefore concentrated their land acquisition elsewhere. They purchased the Perry Ranch near Cache Creek, and then the Kelly Ranch between Clinton and Lillooet, and they also had interests in the Davidson Ranch at 150 Mile House. When Jerome died in 1874, his brother Thaddeus took over all their interests in British Columbia. He was still looking for more land to graze his huge herds of cattle and once again cast his eyes across the Fraser River to the yet unclaimed bunchgrass ranges in the Chilcotin.

Despite numerous accounts to the contrary, it is unlikely that Thaddeus Harper took up land west of the Fraser until at least the 1870s. In 1884, he purchased 18,912 acres of land from the government in the Chilcotin district and established his largest ranch of them all. There remains some mystery as to how the Gang Ranch got its name. Some believe that it was from the large "gang ploughs" that Harper brought in to cultivate the fertile land but, given the rancher's reluctance to put ploughs in the land, that is a bit of a stretch. Others maintain that the ranch was so named from the large gangs of men that were needed to operate the sprawling spread. Whatever the reason for the name, the Gang Ranch became the largest ranch in the province.

Unfortunately, the last ten years of Thaddeus's life were tragic. According to A.W. McMorran, who was the manager of the Gang Ranch in 1939, Thaddeus "was kicked in the face by a horse on his Chilcoten [sic] ranch, which was no doubt the Gang or Harper ranch." Thaddeus never fully recovered from the severe head injuries and died in Victoria in 1898. By then, his lands, amounting to 38,572 acres, had been purchased by the Western Canadian Ranching Company, headed by London publisher Thomas Galpin. The company appointed Galpin's son-in-law, J.D. "Jim" Prentice, to run the Gang Ranch and under his management, the ranch prospered and grew even larger.

Andrew Stobie

ANDREW STOBIE WAS BORN AT Duns in Berwickshire, Scotland, on October 3, 1866, and came to Canada at the age of twenty-one to take care of the sheep operation for the Western Canadian Ranching Company, who operated the Gang Ranch. After five years, he took over the cattle operations of the Gang Ranch as well, and for the next thirty years worked as the operations manager under general manager Jim Prentice.

Stobie was a true character. Harry Marriott, in his book *Cariboo Cowboy*, described him as "a freckle-faced man with square shoulders and large frame, with light brown hair and sand-coloured moustache." Alexander Gillespie, who was also from Berwickshire, worked at the Gang Ranch for Stobie in 1902 and 1903. He recounted the results of Stobie's attraction to hard liquor. Gillespie and a young Indigenous man were mending fences on a Gang Ranch range across the Chilcotin River, and Stobie was along to supervise the operation. However, the Riske Creek store and saloon was only a short distance away, and Stobie's thirst caught up with him. He left the two men to their work and went for refreshment. When the men made camp that evening, there was no sign of Stobie and when morning came, he was still missing. Gillespie suspected the cause of Stobie's absence and rode to Riske Creek, where he found Stobie deep in his cups.

Stobie had been clever enough to ride the old pack horse "Buckskin" to the saloon, knowing that the wise old horse would bring him back to camp, no matter what state he was in, as long as he could stay in the saddle. Gillespie loaded him on Buckskin and started for camp but, about halfway there, Stobie was feeling sick and decided to lay down for a rest. He told Gillespie to tie up Buckskin and go ahead.

That evening, there was no sign of Stobie, and Gillespie thought he must have headed back to Riske Creek. But, as he later recounted, "Somewhere in the small hours of the morning, I was nearly frightened out of my wits by the very irate Stobie grabbing and shaking me violently, swearing like a real cowboy and wanting to know why the ____ I hadn't tied up that ____ Buckskin. I had tied up Buckskin, but that little horse knew that if you keep on pulling at a knot with your teeth, it sometimes comes undone and this one did. Some pack horses know as much as men." Stobie's long walk back to camp had sobered him up but not improved his disposition.

Gang Ranch 1912

HARRY MARRIOTT WAS BORN IN England and came to British Columbia in 1907. After working at odd jobs in British Columbia and Washington State for five years, he took the train north to Ashcroft, intending to find work on a ranch in the Cariboo-Chilcotin. In Ashcroft, he ran into Andrew Stobie, who was in charge of operations at the Gang Ranch and was in town purchasing supplies for the ranch. As the Gang Ranch was 103 miles from Ashcroft, the railway jumping-off spot for the Cariboo and Chilcotin regions, Stobie had brought a huge freight wagon and team of four heavy horses to haul supplies to the ranch and offered Marriott a job at the ranch. Nine days later, on June 7, 1912, Marriott got his first glimpse of the famous ranch, which he described in his book, *Cariboo Cowboy*:

> At the top of a bunch-grass slope the road turned down the sloping hill. What a panorama of size and beauty met my gaze! I saw green hay fields, at least six hundred acres of them, and a cluster of buildings sitting in amidst some native poplar and tall straight Lombardy poplar trees. This was the Gang Ranch, the finest sight any ranch man would ever like to see.

Marriott went on to describe some of the buildings in the ranch headquarters, including "a small lumber house which was the store. In it were supplies of all kinds, from Hudson Bay blankets to plain chewing tobacco." There was also "a large-sized house that was covered with a light tin sheeting and painted red," which was the bunkhouse. By then the Gang Ranch covered some sixty thousand acres of deeded land, plus pastoral land leased from the province.

Marriott's first job at the ranch was breaking workhorses. The huge barn at the ranch had three separate divisions: one for saddle horses, the centre section for workhorse teams, and one for training workhorse colts. Marriott and Jim Ragan, who was in charge of breaking workhorses, started off by getting the young horses used to being handled and put in harness for the first time. Once they were used to this, they would be teamed up with an old, steady workhorse that knew its business and harnessed to a light, strong wagon with a good set of brakes. Ragan would sit on the wagon with the reins, and Marriot would run alongside with a rope from the colt's harness through a strap on its ankle joint. If the colt got too excited, Marriot could pull on the rope and drop the colt to its knees.

The men would work on two colts in the morning and two in the afternoon and, after about a week or ten days, the colts would be used to the harness and the rattle of wagon wheels. With a great deal of patience and gentleness, and the steadying influence of the experienced horse, the colt would be ready for light duty for a time before the real heavy pulling began.

Marriott hauled hay from the Gang Ranch's extensive fields all through the summer and until it was all put in stacks sometime in mid-November. There were about forty-five men involved in putting up hay for the ranch, after which some of them, Marriot included, were employed hauling firewood logs for the next year's wood supply.

The Coldstream Ranch in 1909

THE COLDSTREAM RANCH NEAR VERNON originally controlled about thirteen thousand acres, primarily for raising cattle. But, under the ownership of Lord Aberdeen, then Governor General of Canada, its operation was diversified and it became heavily involved in growing apples as well as raising hogs and sheep alongside the traditional cattle. In the early 1900s, the Coldstream employed about one hundred farm hands in its various activities. As B. Eyre-Walker, who worked for the ranch in 1909, recounted in his book *Rolling On: The Log of a Land Rover* (London: Seeley, Service & Co. Ltd., n.d.):

> There were nine beds in my bunk-house, an upper room in a two-storey building with one window and—being early summer—as hot as the proverbial place. All the beds were occupied in spite of the persistent attentions of bed bugs. That room had for long been disputed property of man and vermin...
>
> "The weather grew warmer and ... I shared a tent with one of the range riders. Many men went under the canvas every summer, so that an encampment of some fifteen or twenty tents sprang up in the scrub that sheltered some of the buildings.

Walker's memories of riding for the Coldstream Ranch are also useful in providing insights into the daily life of the cowboy at the time. Although he was inexperienced, he had done some riding and was chosen to join the working cowboys instead of being placed in any of the other jobs that the Coldstream had to offer. He later wrote:

> In rounding up cattle on the range, a greenhorn invariably got the dirty work—that was part of his initiation. The full-blooded cowboy—the man who had spent a lifetime in perfecting his craft—considered himself among the elite of ranch hands. He had been through the school, yet seldom had the opportunity of bossing others, therefore why should he ride hard after the stragglers that had broken away from the bunch, or flank a herd on a rough hill-side when the valley bottom was smooth and the going easy?
>
> As a greenhorn, I soon found my best friend was my pony. He knew far better than I what a recalcitrant steer meant to do, and if normally clever, thwarted such efforts perfectly. Indeed, given a "cow wise" cayuse, and open country, little remained for the rider to do but stick on. When, however, man and pony were engaged on close work, such as cutting out, roping, etc., the rider's knowledge had to be no less, and every bit as swift in execution as that of his mount, otherwise the twain were soon parted. To expedite this, the methods perfected by riders to guide their mounts were reduced to the greatest simplicity and speed. To the Westerner the reins were not used as a check. To stop, the rider simply threw his weight back in the saddle; to go forward, the reverse. A deviation from the direct course was effected as easily; the swing of the reins meant more to a cayuse than hard pulling on the bit meant to an Old Country hack. Only those who have ridden and worked these clever brutes, can fully appreciate their knowledge of their duties.

<<< **13** >>>

Ranchers

John Wilson, Cattle King

JOHN WILSON WAS BORN IN 1832 at Crossfields Farm near Ravenstonedale, a village in Cumbria in the northwest corner of England. At the age of 17, Johnny travelled to North America, ending up in Logansport, Indiana, in 1849, where he met his future lifelong friend, Lewis Campbell, who was destined to share his fortunes and successes. The young men spent two years working on a farm in Indiana before deciding to try their hands in the goldfields of California.

They heard about the gold discoveries in British Columbia and, in 1858, they headed north with the other gold seekers from California and Oregon, all dreaming of making their fortune. Never afraid of hard work, Wilson engaged in trading on the Fraser River and then once more turned to prospecting, eventually ending up on the famous Tinker Claim on Williams Creek. After two seasons, this immensely successful claim had provided him with the capital to set himself up in a more steady line of work. Noticing that beef was selling for a dollar a pound at Williams Creek, he decided to exploit his experience in the cattle business. He once again linked up with Lewis Campbell, who by then had set himself up on a small ranch on the South Thompson River, east of Fort Kamloops. The two men went into partnership, and, in 1865, travelled to Oregon to purchase a herd of cattle. Campbell's ability to handle cattle, coupled with Wilson's shrewd business sense and eye for good cattle, made for an excellent combination, and the two men were very successful in the booming years of the Cariboo gold rush.

The partners originally held their cattle on Campbell's land on the Thompson, but Wilson saw the potential for ranching in the lush bunchgrass ranges of the BC Interior and began to purchase land there. He initially took up land at Eight Mile Creek in the Cache Creek valley, a few miles north of Ashcroft. By 1897, he owned 1,000 acres there, and in 1868 he acquired 160 acres of good land at Grande Prairie (now Westwold). A few years later, he increased his holdings at Grande Prairie to 1,200 acres of excellent grazing and hay land.

Wilson married a Shuswap woman named Nancy, and the two had a large family. Nancy had been involved with her people in gardening on the meadowlands near Savona's Ferry, known to this day as the Indian Gardens. Wilson purchased this land and added to it over the years until it totalled 1,400 acres. They called the property Indian Gardens Ranch, and the Wilsons occupied it for part of the year, spending the rest of the year on their land near Cache Creek.

Although John Wilson was not an overtly religious man, he was a strong believer in the faith of his forefathers and in the moral code it represented. He believed the church had a place in the community and, as Savona didn't have a church, he sought to rectify the situation. He provided a site and the cost of construction for the building of an Anglican church, asking only that it be called St. Hilda's, which was a common name in the English counties of Westmoreland, Durham, and Yorkshire.

Wilson was a shrewd buyer of cattle. During the 1870s and 1880s, he would ride up the Cariboo road and into the Nicola Valley with saddlebags full of gold coin and gold dust. The jingling of this coin in his saddlebags was a strong incentive to those with whom Wilson was dealing. Keeping the jingling in the background, he would ride through the herd for sale and cast a keen eye over the cattle. Joe Walters, who used to ride with Wilson, told of these sales:

> Johnny'd ride through a bunch of animals with the owner, and point out the old cows and scrubby steers one after the other, and shake his head dolefully. He'd never let on he saw the fat stuff at all, but he did, all right. He'd make a fair enough offer for the lot, but never what the owner expected.
>
> When Johnny made his bid, though, he stayed with it. His word was good. There weren't many cattle buyers in his day, and he could have boosted his profits plenty, but he believed in letting the other fellow have his fair share. At that, Johnny Wilson did all right.

Johnny's saddlebags full of gold were common knowledge throughout the Cariboo, and it was only a matter of time until some desperados decided to relieve him of the extra weight. He usually rode alongside a cowboy for extra protection, but on one occasion the cowboy had dropped some distance behind when a masked horseman stepped out of the woods on some lonely Cariboo road and demanded the saddlebags. Wilson didn't hesitate. Immediately, he let out a wild yell and put his spurs to his horse. He wasn't scared, just smart. He realized he could get away safely before the thief could wheel his horse around. He was out of sight before the robber could sneak back to the Jack pines with the cowboy in hot pursuit.

By the 1890s, as good roads and banks became more common, Wilson exchanged his saddlebags of gold for a suitcase of money carried in a buckboard. Every summer in the 1890s, he would travel by buckboard to the Chilcotin and buy all the cattle for sale. From there he would drive them to his lands near Savona to pasture them until they were marketable, which sometimes took up to five years. The Wilson drives were notorious for "absorbing" other cattle into the herd as they passed through the open ranges and it was not unusual for the drives to finish up with more cattle than they had started out with.

In the forty years that he sold and raised cattle in the Interior, Wilson became one of the most successful ranchers in the industry and was referred to as the BC Cattle King. He continued ranching right up to the end, dying in the Ashcroft Hospital in 1904.

Lewis Campbell

LEWIS CAMPBELL WAS A GIANT of a man in more ways than one. He was well over six feet tall and had an imposing physical presence but he also stood tall among the early drovers who made their way into the Colony of British Columbia in the 1860s. Campbell was born in Ohio to Highland Scottish parents and moved to Indiana when he was eight. There, Campbell met another young man, Johnny Wilson, with whom he was to spend much of his life in partnership. News of the gold discoveries in California lured them to the Golden State in 1853. But the rich gold seemed to elude them, so when word of the discovery of gold in British Columbia reached them, they packed up and headed north. Campbell was no more successful in finding gold in British Columbia, but he soon made good money packing supplies into the isolated mining camps of the Cariboo. By 1864, he had amassed enough money to look for a more permanent place to settle. He and Johnny Wilson travelled to Oregon and purchased beef cattle, driving them north over the old Brigade Trail through the Okanagan Valley. Campbell settled a few miles east of Fort Kamloops, and Wilson west of Lake Kamloops in the Savona area. Both of the men became extremely successful ranchers. Campbell eventually amassed a herd of 3,000 head of cattle grazing on over twenty-five miles of grasslands east of Kamloops.

Since his ranges extended to the outskirts of Kamloops, there were occasional problems with cattle helping themselves in the townspeople's gardens. The City of Kamloops therefore hired a pound-keeper to impound cattle that were trespassing on town property. Eager to fulfill his contract, the poundkeeper rounded up about fifty head of Campbell cattle that had strayed into the town limits. Campbell was reluctant to pay the fine for so many head and summoned his eldest son, Walter, who was the cattle foreman for the ranch and acknowledged as one of the best horsemen in the province. Walter was given twenty-five or thirty dollars and told to take his crew of cowboys to town and show them a good time but to come back with the impounded cattle. The cowboys were delighted at the treat and, after spending the money in various Kamloops bars, they headed back for home, coincidentally passing by the cattle pound. It seemed like a good time to try their roping techniques, and darned if a few fence posts didn't come loose when half a dozen good cow ponies pulled on them. The cattle were driven to a far range where they wouldn't bother the good people of Kamloops again, and the cowboys retired for the night, none the worse for wear.

In a strange twist of fate, that same night the CPR train had been held up by the famous train robber, Bill Miner. When the police rode out in the morning to investigate, they found a number of horses sweated up and were sure that they had found the robbers. It took some fast talking on Walter's part to convince them that this was not the case. When they finally assured Police Chief Fernie that they were innocent, the Campbell cowboys saddled up and accompanied him on his search for the robbers.

Thomas Greenhow

TOM GREENHOW WAS IMPRESSED. He got off his horse and walked through the lush bunchgrass, growing waist-high as far as he could see. He turned to his partner, William Coulter, and said with a grin, "I'm going to spend the rest of my life here at the head of Okanagan Lake."

Thomas Greenhow came from Cumberland in the extreme northwest corner of England. He left home in the early 1860s to seek his fortune in the goldfields of the new Colony of British Columbia. When he reached the Cariboo goldfields, he met William Coulter. The two men found that all the promising ground had been pretty much completely staked before they had arrived on the scene. They watched as drovers brought cattle into the goldfields and sold them at a significant profit and decided that there was a better chance to make a living in the cattle business than in mining. They had heard of the fertile Okanagan Valley while they were struggling in the goldfields and decided to check out the area. After coming upon the extensive bunchgrass ranges at the north end of Okanagan Lake, they decided to buy some cattle and settle there.

In the spring of 1867, the two men travelled from the head of Okanagan Lake south to Oregon and purchased cattle in the Willamette Valley. They drove them over the Cascade Range to The Dalles on the Columbia River, where they met up with two other men bound for British Columbia, Cornelius O'Keefe and Thomas Wood. Since they were all heading in the same direction, the men combined their herds and travelled the trail together, arriving at the head of Okanagan Lake on June 15, where they each staked out a 160-acre pre-emption. Before long, William Coulter sold out to Tom Greenhow, and Thomas Wood abandoned his pre-emption and re-established himself at the south end of the lake, which was later called by his name, Wood Lake. Tom Greenhow and Cornelius O'Keefe stayed at the head of the lake and began to amass more land.

A friendly rivalry developed between Greenhow and O'Keefe. Both men acquired more and more land through purchase and pre-emption. The Kamloops *Inland Sentinel* newspaper reported in 1887 that O'Keefe had 8,000 acres and 900 head of cattle, and Tom Greenhow had a slight edge, with 9,000 acres and 900 head of cattle. It also mentioned that, at their ranches "there are two general stores, one for each." It would seem that, after O'Keefe opened a general store on his property and successfully lobbied to become the postmaster, Tom Greenhow decided to open a general store on his ranch a few hundred yards away.

In 1879, O'Keefe's niece, Elizabeth Coughlin, came to visit her uncle on his ranch. She met Tom Greenhow and fell for the dark, handsome Englishman. The two were married and lived in a log house about fifty-five yards from the O'Keefes on ten acres that Cornelius sold to Tom (for full market price, of course).

Thomas Greenhow, never a healthy man, died in 1889 at the age of 51. He was survived by his wife, Elizabeth, and his two children, Thomas Junior and Mary Victoria.

R.L. Cawston, Boss Driver

RICHARD LOWE CAWSTON ARRIVED IN the South Okanagan in 1872 to work for his uncle, William Lowe, who was in partnership with J.C. Haynes in the cattle business near Osoyoos Lake. Cawston worked for Lowe for ten years as his ranch foreman and learned the cattle trade from the ground up. Lowe soon recognized his abilities and made him the "boss driver" on frequent cattle drives over the Dewdney Trail between the South Okanagan and Hope.

A left-handed crack shot with the rifle, Cawston always maintained that the 1873 Winchester was the best rifle ever made, but he also had a gentle side. Susan Allison, a pioneer in the Princeton area, recalled being woken one night by a gentle tapping at her window. It was Cawston calling her to come outside and witness a glorious display of the northern lights. She sat with Cawston and his cowboys and watched for more than two hours. As she later said, "There was no sound but the awed voices of the men. It was like a glimpse of the 'Beauty of the Lord,' and we all felt it to be such."

Cawston appreciated and cared for the Indigenous cowboys who formed most of the ranch hands in the early days. In 1883, when an epidemic of smallpox raged throughout British Columbia, he received vaccine from the government to vaccinate the Indigenous people of the Similkameen and South Okanagan Valleys. When he realized there was not enough to go around, he was forced to use his initiative. He pushed a number of pins through a whisky bottle cork and stuck each one into the pox sore of someone who was already infected. He then inserted the pin into a healthy arm, transferring the infection and effectively vaccinating the man. The result, while not pretty, had the desired effect. Cawston remarked, "They all took and had arms as big as their legs." The epidemic passed by the area with no casualties. For his efforts, Cawston received three hundred dollars from the government, which he promptly invested in a gold watch and chain.

Like many others before him, Cawston worked long enough to be able to afford his own ranch. His former boss, William Lowe, died in 1882 and, in 1884, Cawston bought the "R" Ranch in the Lower Similkameen south of Keremeos. In 1885, he travelled to Stratford, Ontario, and returned with a bride, Mary Ann Peason.

Cawston continued to ranch and was the first choice among the ranchers of the area as trail boss for the numerous cattle drives going east and west on the Dewdney Trail. While the earliest drives went west to Hope and the coastal markets, the 1890s saw regular drives to the new market in the mining communities of the Kootenays. The trail east involved a difficult crossing of the Columbia River at Trail, where the cattle had to be forced into the water and straight across the wide river. Cawston developed a unique technique for dealing with problem steers that panicked on entering the water and would not follow the herd across. He would leave his horse on the bank and dive in alongside the steer, pulling its head under water a few times, which usually sent it bawling after the herd.

In 1903, Cawston left the area and moved his family to Ontario so his children could receive a better education.

Fred Becher

THROUGHOUT THE EARLY YEARS OF the twentieth century, there was a move toward consolidation of ranch properties into large ranches. Even so, the smaller, family-operated ranch was still the norm in the ranching areas of British Columbia. An abiding sense of community and the value of neighbours were important in the lives of the people whose existence was far from easy. There was seldom any question of helping out a neighbour, and those who refused to acknowledge the importance of cooperation and community did not last for long. Every community had its gathering point, usually where the first post office had been established, and there were occasional opportunities for the entire community to gather for social events. In a time when the drudgery of ranch work left little time for relaxation, these were times for people to get up to date on each other's lives and for young people to look for possible spouses.

The gathering place for the Riske Creek area of the Chilcotin was unquestionably Becher's store. Fred Becher, a big, good-looking man, had become postmaster of the Chilcoten (as it was spelled in those days) Post Office in 1894 and remained so for the next thirty years. His store, hotel, and saloon, admirably located on a long expanse of winding dirt roads, soon earned a reputation as the best stopping house in the Chilcotin. The store was very well stocked, and Becher was generous in letting ranchers run a line of credit until they sold their cattle in the fall. Neither did he take a back seat in accepting the new technology that was changing the outside world. In 1912, a telephone line was strung through the Chilcotin and the first phone was installed in his hotel. The following year, he brought a Cadillac motor car into the country, one of the first to navigate the rough wagon roads of the Chilcotin.

The highlight of the year for many Chilcotin residents was the annual week-long race meet held on Becher's Prairie. Becher was doing very well by the time the First World War started, with two hundred head of cattle, a flock of sheep, and a herd of horses. In addition, he owned several excellent hay meadows. But disaster struck in 1915, when his main building, housing the hotel, store, and saloon, burned to the ground. Unfazed by the disaster, he did not hesitate to construct a new, even grander, building using lumber from his own water-driven sawmill. The new stopping house had twenty-two rooms with a private sitting room for women travellers and a "smoking room" for the men.

Becher married Florence Cole, the daughter of an English clergyman, in 1917 and brought her to the new Becher House. The couple lived a life of luxury for a time, with the new Mrs. Becher entertaining visitors with a lace tablecloth and fine silver tea service. Dances at the house were elegant affairs, and the annual Becher Ball brought people in from as far away as Soda Creek and 150 Mile House. Guests stayed in the hotel or camped in the yard. Unfortunately for Fred Becher, the financial strain of rebuilding, coupled with the growing use of the automobile for travel and the coming of prohibition, meant that business declined and debt piled up. When he died in 1935, his finances were a disaster, but his name lived on in the Chilcotin.

Martin Cecil:
English Lord and Cariboo Rancher

IN 1930, A TWENTY-ONE YEAR-OLD Englishman, Martin Cecil, after a five-hour drive along the dusty Cariboo Road, arrived at the small settlement of 100 Mile House. On viewing the dilapidated huddle of buildings that housed the dozen inhabitants of the town, his heart fell. What had he gotten himself into?

Lord Martin Cecil, whose father was the fifth Marquis of Exeter, was born in 1909 at Burghley House, a modest dwelling of some two hundred-plus rooms. So the rundown shacks of 100 Mile must have seemed a long way from his roots. In 1912, his father had purchased the 15,000 acre Bridge Creek Ranch, which surrounded the 100 Mile House. Lord Cecil, after three years in the Royal Navy, agreed to run it. His first task was to construct a reasonable habitation to replace the decrepit roadhouse. He had no experience in construction but, armed with some books on construction methods and with the help of a few local men, he designed and built the 100 Mile Lodge. He even devised a plumbing system for the new building, using a flume that brought water from Bridge Creek into a thousand-gallon holding tank above the lodge. This system had its obvious limitations in that the water in the flumes froze solid during the lengthy Cariboo winter, necessitating the hauling of water from the creek. Cecil also brought in and installed a 32-volt electrical system.

Cecil also took over management of the Highland Ranch, owned by Lord Ederton of Tatton, making a total of 50,000 acres under his control. But he was a good judge of people and hired Alex Morrison to run the 100 Mile and Don Laidlaw to run the Highland Ranch. As the Depression descended on the BC Interior, Cecil faced an even greater challenge: how to keep the huge holdings under his oversight from disappearing in debt. Between them, the two ranches had 2,000 head of cattle and an equal number of sheep, none of them worth much. Cecil decided that the sheep were less valuable than the cattle and sold them off or traded them for hay. As he began to understand the cattle industry, he became more involved in the political end of the system. When the Cariboo Stockmen's Association was formed in 1934, Cecil was vice-president. The following year, he worked closely with George Mayfield in forming a cooperative marketing system that kept the auctioning of cattle in the hands of the ranchers. That led to the establishment of the Cariboo Cattlemen's Association in 1943, with Cecil as its first president. He was also very involved in the small 100 Mile community as the postmaster and Imperial Oil agent. A deeply spiritual man, Cecil established an Emissaries of Divine Light chapter at 100 Mile, from where he was very involved in the leadership of the international movement.

Lord Cecil Martin looked every inch the working rancher, with casual shirt, jeans, and cowboy hat, even when he became the Seventh Marquis of Exeter in 1981. In this position, he had to travel to Westminster to take his seat in the House of Lords. But 100 Mile House remained his home until his death in 1988.

<<< **14** >>>

Into the Twentieth Century

Gold on Granite Creek

IT WAS A SWELTERING HOT day in the summer of 1884. The heat seemed to bring everything to a standstill, with humans and animals all seeking out the shade. On the John Allison ranch near Princeton, the cattle were all on summer range, and aside from a few cowboys looking out for sick or mud-bogged cattle, the ranch hands were free until haying season. Three of the Allison cowboys, Bill McKeon, Billy Elwell, and Harry Hobbes, drew their wages and dressed themselves in their finest for a visit to the nearby town of Oroville, just across the border in the United States. Susan Allison described these cowboys as "three of the best and most cheerful perverters of the truth I ever knew." Their talents for storytelling were no doubt enhanced by their intake of strong beverages, and their visit "to town" was to prove the spark that ignited a gold rush unlike anything British Columbia had seen in a long time.

The cowboys' week of celebration in Oroville was everything they hoped it would be. The three returned to the ranch with empty pockets and aching heads but, with a twinkle in their bloodshot eyes, they told anyone who would listen that life in the Princeton area would not remain dull for long. Sure enough, the next day, a group of miners arrived in the area asking about the "new strike." The miners had seen gold dust that the cowboys had brought to Oroville, which they had boasted had come from a new gold creek. Now, the Similkameen River had been producing fine gold in small quantities for the previous twenty years, but there was certainly no "new strike" that anyone knew about. The cowboys who created the story were, needless to say, reluctant to give any details about their "find," since it was based primarily on hot air and whisky. Nonetheless, the miners decided to try the surrounding creeks and actually managed to find a fairly rich sandbar in the Similkameen River. However, it was nothing to get too excited about.

Most of the miners were hard workers, but one of their number, Johnny Chance, was too lazy to put in a good day's work, so he was relegated to the role of cook. Ironically, his idleness would work to the advantage of disgruntled colleagues. So they made him cook, but as the weather grew hotter, that was too much exertion for him, so his partners gave him a gun and told him to get them a few grouse. He departed and strolled about until near sunset, when he found a nice cool creek that emptied itself into the river. Here he threw himself downhill with his feet paddling the cool water, when a ray of light fell on something yellow. He drew it toward him, picked it up, and found it was a nugget of pure gold. He looked into the water again and there was another, then another. He pulled out his buckskin purse and slowly filled it, then, picking up his gun, he strolled back to camp, where he became a hero and the discoverer of Granite Creek. Word of the discovery soon leaked out to the outside world, and the Granite Creek rush began in earnest early in 1885.

Lord Strathcona's Horse

DONALD SMITH STARTED OUT AS an apprentice clerk for the Hudson's Bay Company and, through hard work and perseverance, rose to be in charge of all the company's lands in North America. Eventually, he left the company to invest in various businesses including railways, becoming one of the major partners in the Canadian Pacific Railway. In this role, he was the man who drove the last spike at Craigellachie in 1885. He became Canadian High Commissioner in London in 1896 and was named a British peer the next year, taking the title "Lord Strathcona."

When Britain became embroiled in the South African War, Lord Strathcona offered to raise and equip a mounted regiment in Canada at his own expense. The regiment, named Strathcona's Horse, was to consist of three squadrons, one to be raised in Manitoba, one in the North-West Territories (present-day Alberta and Saskatchewan), and one in British Columbia. Commanded by Superintendent Sam Steele of the North West Mounted Police, Strathcona's Horse was recruited from the Mounted Police and from the ranches of western Canada. The ranching community of British Columbia was well represented, with Kamloops and the Okanagan Valley contributing a large number of experienced horsemen, mostly hard-riding cowboys.

On March 18, 1900, a total of 537 officers and men and 599 horses sailed from Halifax. The regiment arrived in Cape Town after a rough sea voyage that took the lives of 120 horses. Initially, the British cavalry looked upon the Strathconas with some amusement because they all rode western saddles and carried lassos, part of the standard issue that Sam Steele had insisted upon. However, the ropes proved to be invaluable in capturing wild horses on the veldt (the South African plains), and the ex-cowboys were masters at throwing a loop over the head of bogged horses and pulling them to safety. Perhaps the best demonstration of their cowboy skills came at Paardekop, where a band of five hundred fresh horses from Natal broke out of a *kraal* (Afrikaner for corral) and galloped off across the veldt. With whoops of glee, the Strathconas grabbed their ropes and rode after them, succeeding in lassoing half of them. The remainder were rounded up and driven back to the corral. In return for their cowboy services, which could not have been accomplished without lassos and stock saddles, they were given the pick of the remounts. From then on, the British maintained a healthy respect for these cowboys from "the colonies."

The tenacity, stamina, and initiative of the rugged westerners were ideal to combat the Afrikaners' unorthodox, guerrilla tactics. Because of these qualities and their superb horsemanship, the Strathconas were made scouts for the advancing army and were often the first to make contact with the enemy, resulting in dozens of casualties. Twelve members of Strathcona's Horse lost their lives in action in South Africa.

In January 1901, the regiment was recalled to Canada and returned via London, where they met their patron, Lord Strathcona, and received medals from King Edward VII in person. The regiment was wined and dined in London and went out to the theatre every night, something the simple cowboys found a distinct contrast from their humble lifestyle at home.

Lord Strathcona's Horse (Royal Canadians) is still in existence, even though the horses have been replaced by armoured vehicles. The regiment has recently served in Afghanistan.

The End of an Era

BY THE EARLY 1890S, THE generation of ranchers who had settled on the bunchgrass ranges of the Okanagan Valley and Thompson River areas were reaching old age. Those who had settled during the 1860s and had remained on their land had been able to accumulate extensive land holdings. They had purchased unoccupied Crown Land and bought up neighbouring lands from other settlers who had not been able to survive during the difficult times of the 1870s. By the time there was a rush to settle the land, after the completion of the Canadian Pacific Railway, the most desirable lands were in the hands of these few ranchers. The ranchers were in no hurry to dispose of their lands, despite the pressure from local and provincial governments and from the media. But circumstances were changing, and it was not long before the effects would be felt.

The situation was even more complicated because of the realization that the hot, dry climate of the southern Interior was particularly conducive to the growing of fruit. This was especially so in the Okanagan and along the Thompson River west of Kamloops, where success could be assured by the availability of water for irrigation purposes. The Coldstream Ranch, near Vernon, had been sold to Lord Aberdeen in 1891 and had successfully grown fruit, using irrigation from the abundant lakes in the surrounding high country. It was obvious to all concerned that the value of rich bottomlands for fruit farming was far greater than any value they might have for ranching.

With the completion of the Shuswap and Okanagan Railway to Vernon and Okanagan Landing in 1892, the Okanagan Valley became prime territory for development of small orchard holdings. The ranchers at first held out, hoping that the price of beef would improve and justify their large holdings. But the situation was changing.

Up until 1897, the quarantine regulations governing the import of cattle from the United States had effectively eliminated cattle from entering British Columbia from the south. After the quarantine regulation were lifted in 1897, American beef began to be shipped into the province in greater and greater numbers. This influx of American cattle, and the resulting lowering of prices, was compounded by the increased number of cattle being shipped in from Alberta. The large ranching companies, such as the Douglas Lake Cattle Company, the Western Canada Ranching Company, near Kamloops; and the British Columbia Cattle Company in the South Okanagan, were able to compete because they had their own butcher shops in the Lower Mainland. But the smaller ranches were faced with lower prices and declining demand for their beef. The difficulties this brought about were enough to make many ranchers look seriously at disposing of their land to developers, who were eager to offer top dollar for land close to the rail line.

By the early years of the twentieth century, the end was in sight. Thomas Wood, at Winfield, was one of the first to sell. In 1903, he sold about four thousand acres to C.B. Lefroy, who subdivided it into small lots for fruit growing. The next three years were to see virtually all of the large ranches in the Okanagan sold off to development companies. In 1904, the Lequime family sold almost 7,000 acres to the Kelowna Land and Orchard Company. A number of the other ranchers in the Okanagan Mission (by then called "Kelowna") area sold out that same year. At the same time, Cornelius O'Keefe put up for sale 3,000 acres of land between Vernon and Okanagan Landing by his agents, the Vernon Okanagan Land Company. The largest land transaction in the Okanagan Valley took place in 1905 when Thomas Ellis sold to the Southern Okanagan Land Company over 30,000 acres of land, including about 20,000 acres that Ellis had bought from the estate of J.C. Haynes in 1895. The BX Ranch was the next to go, being sold in 1906 to land developers based in Winnipeg. One of the last big transactions was in 1907, when Elizabeth Greenhow and Cornelius O'Keefe sold their remaining 15,000 acres to the Land and Agricultural Company of Canada, which was supported by Belgian capital.

The same situation applied to the easily irrigated land along the Thompson River. Developers saw the potential for orchards to be grown and looked for available land. The British Columbia Fruitlands Company was formed and, in 1904, purchased the ranch of Andrew Noble, north of Kamloops. In 1910, the company bought the W.J. Roper ranch at Cherry Creek. A.G. Pemberton on the South Thompson sold to the "Sunnysides" syndicate and, in 1908, the Charles Pennie Ranch, near Savona, was sold to the British Columbia Development Association, who subdivided and established the town of Wallachin.

As was the case in the Okanagan Valley, the generation of ranchers in the Thompson River area who had settled the land in the gold rush years were dying off, and their families were unable or unwilling to continue. William W. Chase on the South Thompson died in 1896, and his land was sold off. Johnny Wilson, the "Cattle King of BC," who had held land at Ashcroft, Grande Prairie (Westwold), and Cache Creek, died in 1904, and his holdings were split among his children. Lewis Campbell, west of Kamloops, died in

1911, and other ranchers who had made their names in the early years also were passing away. It was in many ways the end of an era—a time when, through hard work and perseverance, ranchers had been able to build up their holdings and make their fortune.

The men who settled the vast grasslands during the early years are gone, but the bunchgrass persists. While it was overgrazed, ploughed under, and worn down, bunchgrass still exists in pockets throughout the Thompson Okanagan. In the rich bottomlands, there remains little evidence of the great bunchgrass ranges, as farming and development have destroyed what little remained of the native grasses. But on the hillsides and in the cool upland forests, the native bunchgrasses can still be found. The ranchers, who early on saw the danger in overgrazing, have become conservationists and carefully steward what remains of the precious resource. In some areas, bunchgrass has made a comeback, so that today there are cattle in great numbers grazing on this wonderful resource, just as there were in the era of the 1870s when cowboys ruled the range.

<<< **15** >>>

The Cowboy in Popular Culture

Dime Novels

FOR THE PAST 150 YEARS, the North American cowboy has captured the imagination of the world. The cowboy has come to represent the finest qualities of mankind: the freedom of the outdoors, rugged individualism, and the defence of the oppressed. While the actual life of the cowboy was far from romantic, the mystique of the cowboy has made him into a flamboyant figure, larger than life. How did this happen? How did the "dusty little man on horseback" become an icon in popular culture? In this chapter, I will look at the origins of the "cowboy in pop culture" to see how the mystique of the cowboy started and how it carried on from generation to generation.

The first attempts by the mass media in North America to romanticise the men and women who looked after cattle was in the "dime novel." Cheap paperback sensational novels, often dealing with the frontier, had been around for at least thirty years before Irwin and Erastus Beadle began the famous *Dime Novels* series in 1860. Theirs was the first attempt to issue these inexpensive publications in a continuous series at the fixed price of ten cents. The earliest dime novels featured calm, rugged frontiersman as heroes but, before long, the cowboy became the one who rode to the rescue of women in distress or those threatened by villains. Cowboys were seldom depicted handling cattle. Instead, they were kept busy saving fragile heroines in danger of despicable outlaws or "savage Natives." Aimed mostly at young boys, the early dime novels featured violence and gunplay, but the final outcome always showed that Truth and Goodness would triumph over evil. The image of the larger-than-life cowboy began to emerge. One of the most popular was "Texas Jack," actually based on a real working cowboy, John Omohundro, who had been on early cattle drives out of Texas before becoming a scout and buffalo hunter. Dime novels featured female heroes as well, such as *Hurricane Nell—The Queen of the Saddle and Lasso*, published in 1877.

Despite their great popularity, the dime novels were not considered to be literature of a redeeming nature. The *Canada School Journal* of 1880 complained, "One of the greatest powers for evil is the low and degrading writings our boys and girls are reading ... the vendors of these papers place those having pictures of murderers and Indian outrages, etc. in the windows. The children, attracted by these pictures, buy the papers and read the stories. They soon become intensely interested in the stories and in the slang language in which they are written. The boys and girls buy novels of the same or worse tendency for from five to ten cents. These are purchased and devoured, and thus by degrees is formed the habit of reading this pernicious class of writings."

The disapproval of educators did little to slow down the spread of the dime novel, which became the most popular reading material of its day and launched the myth of the cowboy hero for generations to come.

Buffalo Bill Cody

WILLIAM F. CODY, MORE FAMOUSLY known as Buffalo Bill, was born in Iowa Territory but grew up in his father's hometown in Upper Canada, later Ontario. After his father's death, he became a rider for the Pony Express at age fourteen. Later he served as a civilian scout to the US Army during the Indian Wars, receiving the Medal of Honor from the US government. He received his nickname when he had a contract to supply Kansas Pacific Railroad workers with buffalo meat.

In 1869, Ned Buntline, well-known American publisher and writer, met Cody on a train after he had participated in a battle against the Sioux and Cheyenne. Fascinated with Cody's character and history, Buntline featured him in a dime novel, *Buffalo Bill, King of the Bordermen*, published by the *New York Weekly*. By the time of his death in 1917, Buffalo Bill had been featured as the central character in nearly two thousand dime novels and had become one of the symbols of the "wild west" that captivated the imagination of city-bound children and adults alike.

Cody at first was a reluctant actor in a play entitled *Scouts of the Prairie*, which featured himself along with "Texas Jack" Omohundro and James Butler "Wild Bill" Hickok, other dime-novel heroes. The play was panned by critics but well received by audiences, and Cody began to enjoy the spotlight. In 1883, he started his own open-air show, *Buffalo Bill's Wild West*, which toured the country like a circus. It displayed re-enactments of episodes from the West such as the riding of the Pony Express, "Indian" attacks on wagon trains, and stagecoach robberies. The show also highlighted the cowboy as the representative of Western life, although the cowboy was seldom shown handling cattle. Roping and sharpshooting were standard parts of the show, and visitors were exposed to many authentic Western personalities. For example, Sitting Bull and a band of twenty "braves" appeared, and Cody's headline performers were well known in their own right. People like Annie Oakley and her husband, Frank Butler, put on shooting exhibitions along with the likes of Gabriel Dumont, the famous Canadian Metis, who had fought with Louis Riel.

In 1893, the title was changed to "Buffalo Bill's Wild West and Congress of Rough Riders of the World." The majority of the shows ended with an act recreating an attack on a settler's cabin, in which Cody would ride in with an entourage of cowboys on horseback to defend a settler and his family from a band of Indigenous people, also on horseback. After touring North America, in 1887, he took the show to Britain in celebration of the jubilee year of Queen Victoria. The show was staged in London before going on to Birmingham and then Salford, near Manchester, where it stayed for five months. In 1889, the show toured Europe. In 1890, he met Pope Leo XIII. He set up an exhibition near the Chicago World's Fair of 1893, which greatly contributed to his popularity.

By the time the show closed in 1913, Buffalo Bill was considered one of the most recognizable celebrities on Earth, and the myth of the cowboy was firmly established.

The Virginian

A STRONG, SILENT STRANGER RIDES into the lawless lands of the Western frontier, battles horse thieves, deals with dastardly villains, and wins the heart of a schoolmarm. Although this plot has been repeated thousands of times in popular culture, Owen Wister's 1902 novel, *The Virginian*, is where it first appeared in book form. This classic is widely regarded as the first great cowboy novel of the American West, aside from short stories and dime novels. The cowboy hero of the book, like knights of old, lives by a code of honesty and fair play and is a man of quiet courage and a deep sense of honour. Set in the vast Wyoming territory, this masterpiece helped establish the code of the West and its stereotypical characters: the gentle but brave white-hatted cowboy, the pretty spinster from back East, and villains beyond redemption, all of whom have found their place in popular culture throughout the twentieth century. The novel is also considered to depict the first known "shootout" in American literature.

Owen Wister was an Easterner, born in Pennsylvania, who spent several summers in the American West. He first visited Wyoming in 1885 and loosely based this novel against the backdrop of the "Johnson County War" that took place between the established ranchers and small farmers from 1889 and 1893. In the novel, Wister took the side of the ranchers in this confrontation and the hero, known only as "The Virginian," was on their side. The book became a sensation almost overnight, selling more than 1.5 million copies by 1938 and inspiring four movies, a Broadway play, and a television series. *The Virginian* was voted by the Western American Writers in 1977 as the greatest Western novel of all time. Combining action, romance, and atmosphere, it remains a classic of frontier fiction.

What is little known is that the hero, *The Virginian*, has a Canadian connection. It is widely believed that the hero is based upon Everett Cyril "Ebb" Johnson, who was born in Virginia in 1860. He worked for the Powder River Cattle Company and, in the fall of 1886, drove cattle north to what is now Southern Alberta. Johnson was impressed with the country and, a few years later, he moved north for good. After working on a ranch west of Calgary, he became the foreman of the famous Bar-U Ranch, where he met and married Mary Eleanor Bigland from Windermere, England. His best man was a cowboy named Harry Longabaugh, better known as the Sundance Kid, who was in Canada hiding out from the authorities. Later, Johnson worked for various ranches in the area and then as a cattle buyer.

In 1902, soon after the publication of *The Virginian*, Owen Wister sent a copy, inscribed "To the hero from the author," to Ebb Johnson, acknowledging Johnson as the Virginian. In later years, Johnson ran a successful butcher shop in Cochrane, Alberta. But, realizing that his glory days were at an end, he was never really happy in Canada and longed for his home in Virginia. He retired to Calgary in 1923 and passed away in 1946, but the legacy of "The Virginian" lives on.

Tom Mix:
King of the Movie Cowboys

THE FIRST MOTION PICTURE CAMERAS were invented in the 1890s, but it was in 1902 that the full potential of "movies" was first realized. And the cowboy was there at the start. *The Great Train Robbery* was only twelve minutes long, but was considered a milestone in film-making history. Written, produced, and directed by Edwin S. Porter, a former Edison Studios cameraman, it featured a number of what was at the time considered "unconventional" techniques. Porter actually shot the film on location, not in a studio like previous films, and he moved the camera along with the action. He also used the technique of cross-cutting, in which two scenes are shown to be occurring simultaneously but in different locations. And, as if those were not unconventional enough, he hand-coloured some of the key scenes, decades before colour movies were developed. *The Great Train Robbery* is considered to be the first American action film and the first Western. It was to be followed by countless thousands of westerns, featuring the ever-popular combination of action and romance.

Following the tradition of the dime novel and the Wild West show, moving picture producers began to search for a hero who could exemplify the romantic image of the cowboy: a rugged man of the outdoors who rode to the defence of the oppressed. They found him. Tom Mix was the first and, for many years, the greatest cowboy hero to grace the screen. Beginning in 1909, he was in 291 films, all but nine of which were silent. Mix had been the town marshal of Dewey, Oklahoma, and worked at a number of odd jobs in the Oklahoma Territory. He found employment at the Miller Brothers 101 Ranch, one of the largest ranching businesses in the United States. The ranch had its own touring Wild West show, in which Mix appeared. He stood out as a skilled horseman and expert shot, winning national riding and roping contests at Prescott, Arizona in 1909, and Canon City, Colorado, in 1910.

Tom Mix appeared in over a hundred films for the Selig Polyscope Company and soon became a motion picture "star" on the silent screen.

After the failure of the Selig company, Mix moved on to work for the Fox Film Corporation through the 1920s. The new company featured action-oriented scripts where heroes and villains were easily identified and a clean-cut cowboy always "saved the day." Millions of North American children grew up watching Tom Mix films on Saturday afternoons. His intelligent and handsome horse, Tony, also became a celebrity. Mix did his own stunts and was frequently injured.

Other Western cowboy heroes in the silent moves included Buck Jones, Fred Tompson, William S. Hart, and famous stunt man Yakima Canutt. Through the entire silent movie era, Tom Mix remained the quintessential cowboy and the model for all the movie cowboys who were to follow him. The "King of the Cowboys," as he was acknowledged in his heyday, was killed in a car accident in 1940, but his character, played by actors, was featured on radio programs into the 1950s.

Yakima Canutt:
The Cowboy Stuntman

THE "SILENT SCREEN" MOVIES OF the 1920s catapulted the cowboy into the centre of popular culture. During that era, the majority of actors who portrayed the rugged, virtuous cowboy were experienced cowboys who were excellent horsemen and could perform their own stunts. But one of these silent screen heroes excelled over all the others. Yakima Canutt was born and raised on a ranch in Washington State and broke his first wild horse at the age of eleven. By the time he was seventeen, he had won the title of "World's Best Bronco Buster" and won numerous championships in the next few years. In 1919, after traveling to Los Angeles for a rodeo, Canutt decided to winter in Hollywood. While there, he met many screen personalities, including the "King of the Cowboys" Tom Mix, who invited him to be in two of his movies before returning to the rodeo circuit.

Canutt was invited back to Hollywood in 1923 and worked in eight movies. He proved to be an expert at staging stunts involving horses and perfected the "Crupper Mount," which involved leapfrogging over the horse's rump into the saddle. Famous actor Douglas Fairbanks used some of Canutt's stunts in his 1927 film *The Gaucho* and the two became good friends. In 1924, Canutt broke his nose in the process of doing a stunt that involved falling off a twelve-foot cliff. After a short delay, Canutt continued the movie, thereafter being filmed from the side or back to hide his nose.

By 1928, Canutt had appeared in forty-eight silent movies. But, when "talkies" began to appear, he knew his career was in trouble. He had done damage to his voice while in the Navy in the First World War and was reduced to doing bit parts and stunts in movies. This challenged him to perfect more and more difficult stunts that became staples in the Western movie genre, such as horse falls and wagon wrecks. Canutt developed cables and harnesses that made the stunts safer. Among the new safety devices he invented was the "L" stirrup, which allowed a stunt rider to fall off a horse without getting hung-up in the stirrup. Many of Canutt's most famous stunts could be found in the 1939 classic *Stagecoach* directed by John Ford. His drop-and-drag from a stagecoach, first used in that film, became a standard stunt in Westerns.

While working in Hollywood in 1932, Canutt met a young man named Marion Morrison, who had just taken the stage name John Wayne. Wayne admired Canutt's stunts and asked him to teach them to him. Canutt taught him how to fall off a horse, and the two men developed a technique to make fight scenes more realistic. Much of Wayne's onscreen image , such as his drawling speech and his hip-rolling walk, was copied from Canutt.

Canutt continued to act as a stunt man and supervisor and influenced the portrayal of Westerns for decades to come. He was still working as a stunt expert in 1959 when he staged the chariot race in the first screen version of *Ben Hur*. Canutt taught Charlton Heston and Stephen Boyd to do their own chariot driving and ensured that no animals were injured in the film. Yakima Canutt died at the age of ninety in 1986 and is credited with being the innovator of Western movie stunts and making the cowboy an icon in North American movies.

John Wayne

UNLIKE SO MANY OF THE early cowboy heroes on the silver screen, John Wayne was not raised on a ranch and never worked as a cowboy before becoming everyone's ideal of the cowboy: a man of the outdoors, a rugged individual, and a defender of the oppressed. Wayne was born Marion Morrison and acted under the name Duke Morrison in a bit part in a 1929 movie, *Words and Music*. He was given the name "John Wayne" in a 1930 movie, *The Big Trail*, although he was not even present when his new name was chosen by the director. "John Wayne" went on to become a larger-than-life symbol of the cowboy. *The Big Trail* was the first big-budget Western during the new "talking movies" era, with an enormous $2 million budget, hundreds of extras, and the wide open spaces of the American southwest as a backdrop. While it was a critical success, the movie was a box-office flop and a commercial failure but the name, John Wayne, stuck.

After the failure of *The Big Trail*, John Wayne was reduced to acting bit parts in small-budget Westerns. He became one of the first "singing cowboys" in the 1933 *Riders of Destiny* even though the actual singing was done by someone else and dubbed in. The roll that first pushed him into stardom was John Ford's 1939 epic, *Stagecoach*. After being turned down by all the top movie studios, the film was financed by an independent producer. In the movie, Wayne, who played the Ringo Kid, worked with Yakima Canutt, from whom he learned how to do his own stunts and how to stage fights. Canutt and Wayne pioneered stunts and screen-fighting techniques, many of which are still in use. Much of Wayne's onscreen persona was copied from Canutt. The characterizations associated with Wayne were pure Canutt. Wayne later said, "I spent weeks studying the way Yakima Canutt walked and talked. He was a real cowhand." The film was an unqualified success and catapulted Wayne into stardom. He never looked back.

With the onset of colour movies in the 1940s, Wayne was cast in a variety of roles, most always as the strong, rugged type. But he is best remembered for his western classics: *Fort Apache* and *Red River* (1948); *The Searchers* (1956); *Rio Bravo* (1959); *The Alamo* (1960); which he produced and acted in); *The Man Who Shot Liberty Valence* (1962); *True Grit* (1969); *The Cowboys* (1972); and his last film, *The Shootist* (1976).

John Wayne rose well above the usual recognition that a film actor achieves and became a symbol of the "cowboy" as portrayed in pop culture. His biographer, Ronald Davis, said, "John Wayne personified for millions the nation's frontier heritage. Eighty-three (out of 142) of his movies were Westerns, and in them he played cowboys, cavalrymen, and unconquerable loners extracted from the Republic's central creation myth."

Acknowledgements

THE BOOK HAS BEEN SIGNIFICANTLY enhanced by the addition of sketches provided by my good friend and fellow cowboy enthusiast, Rob Dinwoodie, to whom I am very grateful. I would also like to thank my wife, Debbie, who carefully proofread the manuscript and proved to be an excellent editor.

About the Author

KEN MATHER has been involved in researching, writing, and interpreting Western Canadian heritage for four decades, working in curatorial, management, and research roles at Fort Edmonton Park, Barkerville, and the O'Keefe Ranch since the early 1970s. He is also the author of four previous books on pioneering, ranching, and cowboy history: *Trail North*; *Frontier Cowboys and the Great Divide*; *Bronc Busters and Hay Sloops*; and *Buckeroos and Mud Pups*.

More Great Books by Ken Mather

Trail North

The Okanagan Trail of 1858–68 and Its Origins
in British Columbia and Washington

Ken Mather

PRINT ISBN 978-1-77203-230-7
EBOOK ISBN 978-1-77203-231-4

Visit us at heritagehouse.ca

More Great Books by Ken Mather

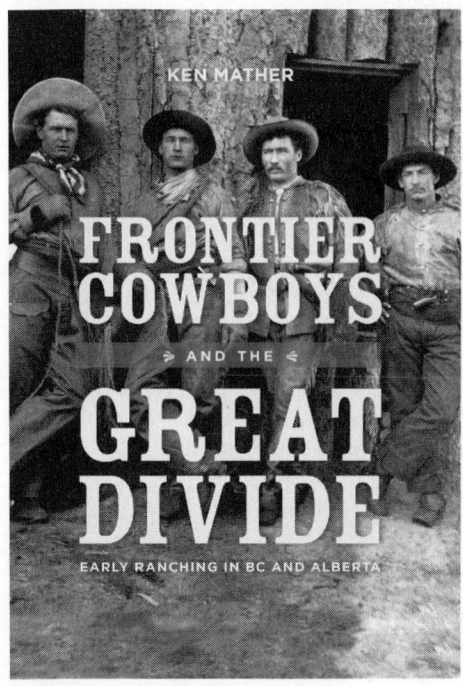

Frontier Cowboys and the Great Divide
Early Ranching in BC and Alberta

Ken Mather

PRINT ISBN 978-1-92752-709-2
EBOOK ISBN 978-1-92752-710-8

Visit us at heritagehouse.ca

More Great Books by Ken Mather

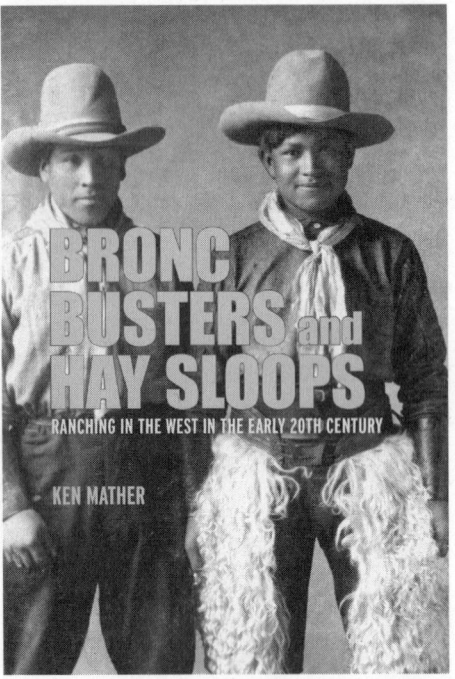

Bronc Busters and Hay Sloops
Ranching in the West in the Early 20th Century

Ken Mather

PRINT ISBN 978-1-894974-92-9
EBOOK ISBN 978-1-926936-68-0

Visit us at heritagehouse.ca

More Great Books by Ken Mather

Buckaroos and Mud Pups
The Early Days of Ranching in British Columbia

Ken Mather

PRINT ISBN 978-1-894974-09-7
EBOOK ISBN 978-1-926936-69-7

Visit us at heritagehouse.ca

More Great Books from Heritage House

Cornelius O'Keefe

The Life, Loves, and Legacy of an Okanagan Rancher

Sherri Field

PRINT ISBN 978-1-77203-248-2

EBOOK ISBN 978-1-77203-249-9

Visit us at heritagehouse.ca

More Great Books from Heritage House

Ranching under the Arch
Stories from the Southern Alberta Rangelands

D. Larraine Andrews

PRINT ISBN 978-1-77203-272-7

EBOOK ISBN 978-1-77203-273-4

Visit us at heritagehouse.ca